The Plain Truth about Living in Mexico

The Plain Truth about Living in Mexico

The Expatriate's Guide to Moving, Retiring, or Just Hanging Out

Doug and Cindi Bower

Universal Publishers
Boca Raton • 2005

The Plain Truth about Living in Mexico

Universal Publishers
Boca Raton , Florida
USA • 2005

ISBN: 1-58112-457-0

Universal-Publishers.com

This book is dedicated to the people of Guanajuato, Mexico, who took us into their hearts and lives as though we were their long-lost cousins who had finally found their way home.

Table of Contents

The Older Language Learner...Mary Schleppegrell, Ph.D

The Downside of Paradise...Bruce McCann

Mexico Living -- A Woman's Perspective...Karen Blue

America's National Culture on the Border...Jacob G. Hornberger

Chapter One
So Long America

What happens when you can no longer afford to live in your own country? You find one where you can and move there.

Shortly after my wife and I moved to a small town in the heartland of Mexico, the idea of writing a book about the *why* and *how* we carried out such a brazen feat occurred to us.

Before the move, the thought that we could pack up, sell everything we owned, say goodbye to family and friends, and leave the country of our birth seemed overwhelming. Most people who expatriate to Mexico are retirees. Here we were in our late forties. What would we do? What city would we choose in which to live? The details seemed unbelievably complex and involved. Just where does one begin? The more we thought about it, the more we discussed it, the more we became intrigued with the possibility of pulling off such a move.

We convinced ourselves of many reasons for making the move to Mexico. The ineptitude of our government in dealing with the terrorism threat scared us. We were sick to death of American politics. We felt conflicted with the declining American culture.

There was an even more terrifyingly compelling reason to leave America. We wondered if we would ever be able to afford to retire in our own country.- Even more horrible was we were quickly becoming unable to afford life in America in the present! Besides, if ever there was a good time to make this move, if indeed we were going to do it, it was while we were still reasonably young.

Therefore, in the fall of 2001, we began doing research to see if moving to Mexico was an alternative for us. We had to find out if it was affordable to live there. We had to unlock the mystery of moving to another country, so we hit the Internet.

If you will permit me to digress, I will explain what happened that caused us to be unable to afford to live in our own country. This is of interest to almost everyone we meet here, expats, and Mexicans alike. It is the number-one question people ask us on learning that we are full-time residents of this wonderful country.

Is it not everyone's worst nightmare to become afflicted with some hideous disease? And you don't have just any disease, but one that confounds not only your personal doctor, but also every brilliant medical mind in the medical community? After enduring every medical test known to medical science, your doctor sends you to every specialist in a four-state region. Through all this, you spend enough money in travel and co-pays to fund ten scholarships to Harvard Medical School. Finally, someone realizes what you have and you get the call!

In May 1994, I got such a call from my doctor. My nightmare had become a reality. I had been ill for about two years with some strange and inexplicable flu-like illness from which I have *never* recovered. I had flu-like fatigue and muscle pain that would not stop, ever. With it, I had sleep disturbances. I could never get a restful night's sleep. Now I had a diagnosis. Sitting across from my doctor at his desk, waiting to hear the bad news, I was sure I was dead meat. What in God's name was wrong with me?

My doctor calmly told me that I had an illness called *Fibromyalgia Syndrome.* The good news was that it wasn't lethal. The bad news was the symptoms would be unrelentingly severe, probably debilitating, and would afflict me with lifelong pain, fatigue, and sleep disturbances.

For those who are interested, Fibromyalgia Syndrome, or FMS, is a chronic, incurable, but not terminal, pain, fatigue, and sleep disorder. It is an illness of unknown causes. The disease includes a host of symptoms. There is numbness and tingling in the extremities, severe headaches, and anxiety (and just who wouldn't be anxious at this point?). There is also some dastardly beast called Irritable Bowel Syndrome (don't even ask me to explain that one!). If that wasn't frightening enough, I learned that it is an illness that afflicts mostly women! I could not win.

I must say, to the doctor's credit, that he tried to soothe my fears. He answered all my questions, loaded me up with a ton of literature, and then reminded me to pay my co-pay on the way out... "Next patient, please."

The literature painted a hopeful and positive slant to the horror that had just invaded my life. The gist is though Fibromyalgia is incurable; it will more than likely torture me with unrelenting pain. It afflicts me with mind-numbing fatigue so I forget what I am looking for when going from

11

one grocery store aisle to another. It also gives me lifelong sleep deprivation. Though it isn't lethal (it will only make me pray for death), it is treatable; well, more or less.

The skinny on managing this illness is with expensive drugs and avoiding the following: cold, wet weather; hot, wet weather; frequent weather fronts; stress; over-activity, or a sedentary lifestyle. Not bad, you say? Gives someone something to work with, does it? Read on!

We were living in Kansas City when I received my diagnosis. If you know anything at all about the weather in America's heartland, you know that it defines the phrase, *Bad Weather*.

Kansas changes weather fronts more often that some people change their minds. The winters can chill you to the bone. The springs can humidify the skin right off your limbs (or at least give you a bad hair day). The summers offer tornadoes or flooding, which send you screaming for your life at least once a week. Bad weather and stress, in Kansas, are twins.

The year-round weather extremes aggravated my symptoms and kept my stress at stroke levels. The increased stress made the FMS symptoms worse. It became a three-ring circus of pain, fatigue, and sleep disturbances made worse by the weather, which caused more stress, which in turn increased the symptoms--and so it went, on and on.

We considered moving to the Southwest part of the United States, but we found this alternative sadly lacking. However, the weather there offered better symptom control, though there were problems. There are always problems!

The job market in the local economy was bad, to say the least. I could no longer work, of course. My poor, dear wife, try as she did, came up shooting blanks. The jobless economy, high real estate prices, only a slightly lower cost-of-living, and the inescapable rising costs of prescription drugs painted a grim picture. No matter where we would live in America, we could not escape the impossibly high costs of prescriptions--our Achilles heel!

Therefore, we opted to stay put and try plan B in controlling my illness with prescription drugs. There were two pain medications, two sleep medications, one for neuropathic pain, and three others for Irritable Bowel Syndrome. Between 1994 and 2000, I was taking ten medications, all with their own vicious co-pays of $25.00 - $50.00 each. You do the math. My wife was also on two or three prescriptions. We were in a bad position that was not getting any better.

Now, mind you, there were other continuing medical costs: doctor office visits, frequent medical tests, and the cost of the health insurance premiums. The monthly costs were staggering and only added to both of our stress levels.

Our total medical cost was over $500.00 a month and quickly approaching the $600.00 mark. This was so serious and we simply could no longer cope. We couldn't afford to move. The cost of prescriptions was becoming unaffordable. What were we to do? At the time, I didn't have a clue.

We found little comfort that other Americans were struggling horribly to try to afford their prescriptions. I'm not talking people in the low-income bracket who are eligible for government aid. I'm talking about people with incomes and even insurance who can't afford the drugs their doctors prescribe.

It turns out more than 50% of bankruptcies filed in 2001 were medically related and involved middle-class homeowners who not only had an income, but also health insurance. The prevailing myth that most bankruptcies are due to credit card debt is not true. Less than 1% of filed bankruptcies are because of credit card debt.

Doug & Cindi Bower

Researchers found that in those surveyed, 1.9 to 2.2 million U.S. residents filed a "medical bankruptcy". The average person filing for bankruptcy during the 2001 period spent $13,460 on co-payments, deductibles, and uncovered services even though they had private insurance.

"Our study is frightening. Unless you're Bill Gates, you're just one serious illness away from bankruptcy. Most of the medically bankrupt were average Americans who happened to get sick. Health insurance offered little protection," said Dr. David Himmelstein, an associate professor of medicine at Harvard Medical School who led the study.

Another one of the study's authors, Elizabeth Warren, said, "It doesn't take a medical catastrophe to create a financial catastrophe. A larger share of American workers is going to have insurance that's like a paper umbrella. It looks good, and it might even protect you in a sprinkle, but it melts away in a downpour."

A 2003 study found that those above the poverty level suffered a greater out-of-pocket expense trying to afford medical costs not covered by insurance. They had an income, although it was low, but had greater difficulty meeting co-pays than those who were below the poverty line. Those below the poverty line had the advantage of being eligible for Medicaid to pay their medical costs. Those at or slightly above the poverty line suffered the most. They made too much money to be eligible for Medicaid, yet did not make a high enough income to afford uncovered medical costs.

A retired Wisconsin couple went into shock when they discovered that their pharmacy bill for the year was higher than their annual real estate tax bill. Not only was that a shocker, but they stopped carrying prescription coverage because their annual premium equaled the benefits to the tune of $6,000 a year. Can you imagine that? This desperate couple began looking to Canada for their prescription needs.

Somewhere in the dark and dank abyss of the Kansas winter of 2001, desperation, despair, dread, or all three, drove me to look for alternatives to buy the drugs we both needed. I was, to be honest, a bit nervous (terrified) about ordering drugs online and from another country. Desperation overcame my fears.

To my shock and amazement, I learned that not only could we buy cheaper prescriptions from Canada, but also from Mexico. Mexico was the less expensive of the two. One little website led to another, revealing that not only were prescription drugs cheaper in Mexico, but so was just about everything else. Life itself was cheaper in Mexico!

Call me a dull-wit, a half-wit, or a nitwit! During that decade of horrible financial struggle to pay for the drugs I needed for my FMS, it never once dawned on my Fibromyalgia-weakened brain that Mexico could have been an affordable alternative. It is affordable, not only for prescriptions, but also as a place in which to live. It must have been the FMS that dulled my normally superior intellect. Yes, that was it.

We discovered that my Social Security Disability pension, though small, could support us comfortably in Mexico. In America, my pension barely covered our medical costs and a few, and I mean a few, necessities. In Mexico, my pension would be more than twice that of a middle-class family's income. It would cover not only our medical costs, but also almost all of our cost-of-living expenses.

I should make the point the "How to Retire to Mexico" books on the market might argue with what I've just written. Some would argue the cost of living isn't that different. If you come to Mexico and settle in one of the popular 'Gringo Land' areas, you may find your cost-of-living expenses as high as or even higher than they were in the USA. However, if you live in a town like Guanajuato, where we live, you probably will find your cost of living is lower than in the USA. If you come to Mexico expecting to live like the Queen of Sheba, then it is going to cost you--a lot!

What I am saying is that you can live well on little if you move to a genuine Mexican town and live like a native. If you move to an "Americanized" Mexican town, your costs will be higher. Still, they will most likely be less than they were in the States.

We moved to a university town of about 100,000. It is a small, genuinely Mexican town. We have lower prices on almost everything you can imagine. Our rent, utilities, and a maid cost about $5400.00 pesos a month. At today's exchange rate, that is about $488.00 USD a month. We live in a quiet, safe location on the side of a mountain with a marvelous view. We have a lovely two-bedroom house, phone, patio, and a washer. Not only did the heartland of Mexico meet our financial need crisis, it also offered us a year-round stable climate in which to manage my chronic illness.

Here in Mexico's heartland, at 6500 feet, we have an almost perfect climate. It is a paradise of sorts. It is "eternal springtime". The temperatures are ideal and the weather is wonderful almost year-round. During the rainy season (mid-May to mid-September), I do have to cope with some weather fronts which can aggravate my illness. However, if I had to choose year-round symptoms as opposed to 3-4 months of symptoms, well, it's a no-brainer.

We've become self-appointed gringo ambassadors here in our little adopted town of Guanajuato. The bizarre habit we've developed is that when we see fellow gringos, we walk right up to them and introduce ourselves.

"Hi! I am Doug and this is my wife, Cindi. Who are you and where are you from?"

I know some people would consider this a little strange and perhaps a bit psychotic if practiced in the United States. I do recall Americans practicing this courtesy regularly in the past. However, from the reactions we get from those we dare to accost with our rash and brazen friendliness, I think that it is a custom long gone from American culture. But anyway.

After the shock wears off, we exchange personal information. The second shock sets in when we tell them that we are living in the city in which they are standing, talking to us.

From *that* reaction, you would think that I had just slapped them in the face. Or perhaps that I had revealed to them that my wife and I were quadruple ax-murdering serial killers wanted by the FBI and by four other countries. Thankfully, that shock wears off quickly. When it does, they regale us with questions about the who, what, when, where, why, and how of our expatriation to Mexico. And oddly, some of these gringos are so interested that they've taken us, total strangers, to lunch to grill us on details. Many have confessed to us that they too have been thinking about such a move and need details...lots of information!

Americans expatriate to Mexico for various reasons. Employment, marriage into a Mexican family, to study Spanish, the climate, or to expose the children to a new culture are some. There are a few who expatriate for nefarious reasons that I shall not reveal because the reasons are, well, nefarious.

When telling those close to you of your decision to move to Mexico, their reactions can border on the hysterical. Our family and friends all had to share some horribly gruesome story about Mexico on hearing of our decision. Everyone thought it his or her solemn duty to tell us what would happen to us because of what had to be an insane decision to move to a third-world country.

Why do Americans think they have to do this? Why does the mere mention of Mexico evoke such fear and trembling in the minds of Americans? I mean, we are talking strong emotions when it comes to the subject of Mexico. The real kicker of it is that most of those with hair-raising stories, warning us of immediate death should we put one toe over the American-Mexican border, have never even been to Mexico. However, they all have stories! And what do they hope to accomplish with these stories? They act as though we woke up one morning and said,

"Hark! I have an irrational thought. Let's move to Mexico. Why don't we tell our family and friends of our impulsive and rash decision?"

Perhaps they think these stories will somehow scare us into repenting of what has to be, in their thinking, irrationality. I know of no expat who did not take years to research and think about the decision to expatriate before making the move (we spent three years in research). Have I been on a diatribe? Oh my, and so early in the book! Moving on.

So, why are we here in Mexico? It's the great climate, wonderful people, and affordable living. *How* did we carry it out? I hope to answer that question in the rest of this book. The plan of this book is simple. We hope to share with you what to expect in the details of daily life in Mexico. The biggest shock we met in coming to a foreign country to spend the rest of our lives was not the language or culture of Mexico. It was, rather, seeing how Americans act in this country.

Americans have a bad worldwide reputation and, from what we've seen of their behavior in some of the popular 'Gringo Land' towns where they congregate, they deserve the reputation. We hope to address those issues and offer solutions.

On August 1, 2003, we stepped off the plane in Leon to begin this adventurous new chapter in our lives. We've never looked back and have missed little in the United States (we do miss Starbuck's white chocolate Mocha!).

Chapter Two
Ugly American Syndrome

Are you feeling a bit inspired at this point? Have you too felt similar worries that you also might not be able to afford to retire in the land of your birth? Perhaps you can't afford to live there now. Or, perhaps you have grown sick and tired of the trap you feel you are in and want out. Maybe you need something new and challenging and perhaps, just perhaps, Mexico is something worth considering.

"Can I too pull off a move to Mexico?"

The short answer to that question is yes. I believe anyone can find a niche in which to live in Mexico. I feel there is, whatever your financial status, health or climatic needs, a place just right for you.

The long answer is that you had better think about this for a very long time.

The decision to move to Mexico cannot be rash or

impulsive. To move on a whim could be disastrous. Before moving to Guanajuato, we took a full three years to examine the possibility. We did research online, read books, talked to expatriates via chat rooms and e-mail, and even made a fact-finding trip to the city we had chosen as a potential home. You must take all the time you need to become 100% sure that expatriating to Mexico is right for you.

One reason for all this research is that Americans have traditionally been clueless about other countries and cultures. Most Americans haven't had the opportunities Europeans or even those in the American-Mexican border towns have had to interact with foreign cultures.

A good example of what I mean is if you were a New Yorker and had to move to El Paso or Laredo, Texas, you would find an un-American culture there! Because of their nearness to Mexico, you would find, for all practical purposes, Mexican towns. We've been to El Paso and Laredo many times and they are Mexican towns on American soil. The last I heard, only 20% of El Paso's residents are bilingual, the other 80% speak nothing but Spanish. Can you imagine living in a town like that? It is thoroughly Mexican. As a New Yorker, as American as anyone in El Paso or Laredo, you would find a new and different culture. You would have some cultural issues that you would need to work through.

The American-Mexican border towns are very different from the rest of America. They are different from the rest of Mexico, though they are Mexican in nature. I am convinced that anyone living in any of these border towns could move into the interior of Mexico and have few problems adapting to the culture. But, with the rest of America not lucky enough to live that close to Mexico, many Americans are clueless about what Mexico is like.

You've got to think long and hard about expatriating,

especially if you are not familiar with Hispanic culture. Mexico is not America! You can't come to Mexico, even for a visit, and expect this country to adapt to your American expectations and wants. It just won't work! You have to get this into your head. Your survival in this culture as an expatriate depends on you adapting to it and not the other way around. Mexico is not America – don't forget this!

It doesn't take long to tell which gringos came from towns with large Mexican populations and those who did not. All you have to do is sit and watch for the tight, solemn, and anal expressions on gringos' sour faces. Listen to how loudly and rudely they speak. Listen to the demands they make and the fits they inevitably pitch, to tell which ones are the culturally challenged Americans. Why do they bother to come here? Why waste their money coming here if they are going to act like that? We see this behavior constantly!

I think the average American comes to Mexico expecting every city to be a resort town like Puerto Vallarta or Cancun. I think they believe, and genuinely so, the entire country is customized to their tourist expectations. All of Mexico is not like the resort towns--and thank God for that! You would think the phrase "Mexico is not America" should be a bit self-evident. But by the way many gringos act in Mexico, seemingly, that piece of self-evident logic has passed them by. To put it in the words of a Mexican national:

"Why do you Americans come to our country if you are going to act so unhappy?"

Sadly, this is exactly what we've seen in many of our fellow gringos. And I think it is because of false expectations of what Mexico is as a country and culture. We have met expats here in Guanajuato who began their expatriation adventures in other towns with larger gringo populations. These people would regale us with horror stories of the behavior of the gringos. This, finally, was their reason for leaving and moving to Guanajuato.

Because these stories seemed so horrific, we decided to see for ourselves rather than accept these tales from third parties. So, we packed up and went to one of the cities that has a large gringo population for a few days. Our plan was to sit in the plaza and simply watch the gringos interact with the locals. We also planned to talk to the local Mexican residents to see how they felt about how the gringos treated them and gringo behavior in general. We planned this little fact-finding trip to collect information for this book.

It did not disappoint us.

Mexican cities have wonderful plazas. Usually there is a main plaza with smaller ones strewn throughout the city. These plazas are beautiful parks with ample shade trees, benches, and restaurants. They are great places for sitting and doing nothing if you so wish. It is great for de-stressing.

The main plaza, located in the center of this cute colonial town, is beautiful. A magnificent church, some shops, and restaurants ring the square. It is a great location for watching the life of the town. So, there we sat. It didn't take long.

I saw a woman of retirement age talking with a friend when one of the local beggars approached her and begged for a peso. Now, if you know anything at all about Mexico, you know that panhandling beggars are a way of life here. It is ingrained in this culture. It is here to stay and isn't going away anytime soon.

Panhandling beggars are not unique to Mexico. America has its share, as does Europe. Remember what I said about the American-Mexican border towns? El Paso, Texas, has a huge number of panhandling beggars.

Anyway, this old woman came unglued. She began shrieking, in English of course,

"No, no, damn you! I won't give you any money. I want you to give me your money! Give me, give me, give me!"

This beggar woman, obviously used to a simple, "No, gracias" and then moving on to her next mark, ran in horror for her life in the opposite direction with the old biddy in hot pursuit. The old gal chased this beggar across the plaza and down the block continuing to screech, "Give me your money!"

The old crow, who couldn't keep up with the more fleet-of-foot beggar, finally gave up the chase and returned to her friend, laughing triumphantly that she would begin performing this new civilized behavior of hers regularly. This led me to believe that perhaps she was an expat or at least a long-term seasonal resident. We don't need nor want Americans who act like that here--please go away, thank you very much!

My wife personally witnessed a man and his companion sitting on an unusually long bench with several Mexican nationals, discussing in excessively loud voices how cruel Mexicans are to their dogs.

And the list goes on!

A gringa (female gringo) enters a bank and begins screaming like a banshee:

"I know some #%$* employee speaks English here and I want to talk to them right now!"

What wonderfully mature behavior we gringos show our Mexican hosts who graciously allow us to live in their country!

Then, there was the woman who refused to get out of a cab until the cabbie accepted her American dollars. I am not making this stuff up!

An incident I saw right here in Guanajuato involved a tour group of retirees. They were standing around listening to their guide drone on. Suddenly, an old woman broke formation and marched up to a Mexican mother who had just given her child a torta (a sandwich) for breakfast. In her best haughty American indignation, she began chewing this mother out (in English of course) about her selection of breakfast foods for her child.

I am compelled to ask, "Just who do Americans think they are?" Just who gave them permission to come to someone else's country and act like this? Talk about an inflated sense of entitlement!

Here is what I mean when I say you had better think twice about expatriating (or even vacationing) to Mexico. If you are offended by panhandling beggars or by the way Mexicans treat their animals, then don't come here. If you expect everyone here to speak English, don't waste your time coming here. If you are too lazy to change your dollars to pesos, then don't waste your money coming here. If you don't approve of what Mexican mothers choose to serve their children for breakfast, then don't bother to come here!

Now, lest you think I am being too harsh, mean-spirited, or anti-American, let me assure you I am not. Neither I, nor my wife, are anti-American. We are Americans, born and bred in the United States of America. So, if we were anti-American we would be anti-us. Is that even possible? I don't know. Anyway, why the rancor?

Our dismay and dread is not with individual gringos. It is with the horrible disease that afflicts 99% of the American public. It is a serious illness that you should not take lightly. However, it is curable. Fittingly, its name is:

The Ugly American Syndrome

This is a horrible disorder which afflicts most of the people in the United States. It has as its cause a culture that breeds egocentricism and narcissism. The culture breeds a false and excessively inflated sense of entitlement to having life handed to one on a silver platter. It breeds culture-centric false superiority and an overwhelmingly arrogant and inflated sense of one's own importance.

One can express the symptoms anywhere, anytime, or in any country--even in one's home country. This affliction is not limited to foreign travel or living abroad. The symptoms are as follows:

The Ugly American Syndrome produces the attitude that America has the most superior culture on the face of the earth. It also produces a wish to Americanize everything that one finds in foreign cultures.

The Ugly American Syndrome produces contempt for other languages. It also produces the sentiment that every country on the planet should speak English. It also causes the false opinion that 52% of the world is English-speaking when in reality less than 20% is English-speaking.

The Ugly American Syndrome produces loud talking, demonstratively stupid Americans, who want to be the center of attention in every circumstance.

The Ugly American Syndrome produces a total malaise in absorbing even a shred of another culture.

The Ugly American Syndrome produces an anger control problem. Some people display rage behavior if Mexicans don't conform to American expectations.

The Ugly American Syndrome causes the belief that an American is free to mistreat, threaten, insult, or hate anyone who isn't an American.

The Ugly American Syndrome produces an American who has the idea that courtesy, humility, politeness, and long-suffering don't apply to him.

The Ugly American Syndrome produces chronic complaining, troublemaking, fight starting, and confrontational behavior.

The Ugly American Syndrome produces an extreme paranoia of all cultures, especially Mexicans. Some people have the belief that foreigners will always cheat you, rob you, or plunder and pillage you at every opportunity.

The Ugly American Syndrome produces a marked sense of denial there is anything wrong with one's behavior. It allows one to act like a jackass in another country or when interacting with a foreign visitor in America.

As you can see, this is a horrible illness that Americans carry all over the world. Fortunately, it seems, it is a disease that afflicts only American and some Canadians.

I simply cannot fathom what gets into the minds of Americans who seemingly give themselves permission to regard the rest of the world as their subservient. I simply cannot grasp this. Perhaps it is America's own unique humanist worldview that allows them to act like Ding Dongs in foreign countries.

As I mentioned, there is a cure for this rather nasty behavioral disorder. There are practices that you can adopt to begin reversing the effects of the Ugly American Syndrome:

Practice generous amounts of kindness, humility, generosity, long-suffering, and patience. This will force Mexican nationals to have to guess the real country of your origin.

Don't walk around public places with fists full of cash. Don't tell everyone how filthy rich you are and where you are staying. Don't invite them to come to your room and have a drink with you.

Keep insulting, childish thoughts, such as the following, to yourself:

- Where's the satellite TV?
- You call this beer?

- My goodness, these women are fat!
- Is it always this filthy in Mexico?
- This country would be great if it weren't for all the Mexicans.
- Do you know your government is corrupt?
- Why can't you do things like Americans?
- I know everyone here speaks English.
- You call this a taco?
- I asked for cash, not pesos.
- How much is that in real money?

Something else you can do to reverse the Ugly American Syndrome effect is to try to speak Spanish. This will throw Mexicans off about your secret identity.

Mexican happiness and helpfulness are plentiful traits in this country's culture. Though about 42 million Mexicans are dirt poor and live in terrible poverty, making less than one dollar a day, there is more happiness here than whining and complaining over what they don't have materially. They decide to enjoy life rather than allow dire circumstances to overwhelm them. Their faith and trust in Almighty God rules this culture, no matter the circumstance. I rather like that and hope it never changes.

America could learn a lot from this third-world country-- a heck of a lot!

It was next to impossible to get most of the Mexicans we interviewed in this town to talk about the manner in which the gringo population treats them. You could tell that they wanted to say "something", but felt uncomfortable in doing so. They knew which side of the bread gets buttered and by whom! If everything was peachy-keen, you would have assumed they would have said so. They didn't. I think that perhaps a formal written survey would have been less threatening or intimidating and a better way to go.

Cab drivers were just about the only people who would talk to us. They were frank and pointed out the gringo presence had improved the standard of living for many Mexicans because of the money poured into the economy. However, they were insulted because *most* (the word they used) of the gringos would not associate with the Mexican nationals. Also, the gringos did not appear to want to learn Spanish. We had long suspected this, but feel we need more survey responses to support the claims of the few who did talk to us. We plan to do a more comprehensive survey for another book. We will re-survey this town as well as other cities with large expat populations.

The authors think the probable cause of the weak association the locals have with the American population is because of the Americans' lack of linguistic skills. If the Americans would bother to learn the language, then communication could begin to strengthen the ties between the two groups. As long as the vast majority refuses to learn Spanish, there will be a communication blackout in social affairs. How can you even begin to work on problems if you cannot talk to each another? This town will be doomed to having a split personality socially until the Americans wake up and understand that this is not *their* country, but that it belongs to the Mexicans.

Acting like The Ugly American is not the solution!

Chapter Three
Crime

There are many subjects about Mexico that make women gasp and men click their tongues. Crime is the issue that causes the most apprehension.

It appears that every American is an expert in Mexican International Relations. Everyone delights in telling gruesome stories of murder and mayhem that happen in Mexico.

Picture this scene:

"Well, Brother," I say, as we pull into the driveway of my brother's million-dollar home, "the wife and I have decided to move to Mexico."

"Mexico! Are you crazy?" he shouts.

Having exited the car, I gather my wits to launch a counterargument. He interrupts. "Before you comment, let me be sure to set the car alarm."

We approach the house and once again I try responding but he chimes in, "Hold that thought while I deactivate the house alarm."

The house alarm deactivated, we enter, and he quickly resets the alarm. He rushes out the back door to release the Doberman guard dogs.

He reenters the living room with a couple of beers.

"Ok, where were we? Mexico? Isn't it dangerous down there?"

In the research stage of trying to discover if Mexico was right for us, we learned two pieces of information about the issue of crime. First: Americans have an irrational fear of crime in Mexico. Second: There *is* crime in Mexico.

Crime should be a concern for everyone, no matter where on the planet you live. If you want to expatriate, you need to wrestle with this issue until you come to an understanding and a coping level for you. In other words, if you don't find a comfort zone with this issue, don't think of moving to Mexico.

The problem with Americans is they seem to have the most hideously gruesome Texas-chainsaw-massacre understanding of crime in Mexico. They are tall yarns that are rarely, if ever, based on fact.

It is our strongest recommendation that you become satisfied with this issue long before stepping foot on Mexican soil. Not to do so will leave you conflicted, scared, and unhappy.

Let me reiterate, there *is* crime in Mexico. There is crime because Mexico is full of the same kinds of people we have in the United States: imperfect and fallible. They screw up just like we do and some make bad decisions in their behavior and, in doing so, break the laws of God and man.

Crime in Mexico will, as in any other place in the universe, wax and wane in intensity. Sometimes there will be a low crime rate and sometimes not. It is an imperfect place in which to live. If it were perfect, I surely would have destroyed its perfection when I moved there since I am not perfect.

The fact of crime in Mexico isn't what vexes me so. What causes me no end of vexation is how some xenophobic Americans will point out just how dangerous they perceive Mexico to be. They act as if it is their Constitutional duty to tell you just what a mistake you are making in wanting to move to Mexico.

"Oh, I have this friend who went to Vallarta once who talked to this waiter who told her he talked with this guy who knows a woman who heard this story..."

For an *American* to get his boxer shorts all twisted in a knot over crime in Mexico is, well, silly! According to one of the online almanacs, aneki.com, the U.S.A. ranks in the top sixteen most dangerous countries in the world. Mexico did not even make the list!

Do you recall these?

Littleton, Colorado: Two crazed gun-toting teenagers went on a killing spree in their school. Twelve students and a teacher left dead.

In Texas, two white men tied a black man to the back of their pickup truck and dragged him to his death just because of the color of his skin.

A white supremacist in Chicago decided his victims didn't belong in a Starbucks, so went on a shooting binge.

A crime occurs every two seconds in the United States. Every three seconds it is a property crime, every four seconds a larceny. Every thirteen seconds it is a burglary. Every twenty-three seconds it is a car theft. Every twenty-eight seconds an aggravated assault occurs. Every sixty seconds someone commits a robbery and every five minutes a rape. Every twenty-nine minutes there is a murder.

This is America I am describing and not Iraq.

The FBI reports in the "old days", law enforcement

solved 91% of the murders. Family members and acquaintances committed the majority. Today, law enforcement solves fewer than 65% of the murders and strangers perpetrate 53% of them. Times have changed, haven't they?

In America, 10 out of 100,000 people will be homicide victims. In 1900, only one out of every 100,000 could expect to become a murder victim.

The point is that one must have a little perspective in evaluating crime in Mexico, especially when one comes from the United States.

"I know someone, who in broad daylight, walked out of a bank only to have someone hit him in the head. The person dragged him to a car, put him in the trunk, and took him out into the desert. There, he stripped him, robbed him, beat him, and left him to walk back to town naked!"

"Mexican police will arrest you just for being an American."

"Taxicab drivers will kill you on the spot."

"Roving gangs will drag you by the hair on your head out of the restaurant in which you are eating and rob you!"

I heard these stories from friends in the United States when I told them that we were moving to Mexico. We are still waiting to hear or see any of these events occur.

You can find sources of legitimate crime reports on the U.S. State Department web site and in popular, current guidebooks. These sources can give possible crime conditions in foreign countries. However, one still must learn to "read between the lines" in these reports. They generalize the facts. Keep that in mind.

One such generalization is in the U.S. State Department's warning about Mexico. It warns of "high levels" of crime against tourists, especially in larger cities.

This warning applies to the larger cities in Mexico and specifically to Mexico City. Take it no further than that! Don't judge all of Mexico based on a generalization about crime in its larger (and largest) cities. You would no more tell a foreigner visiting America that all of America has the same crime problems as Los Angeles. So, don't make the same mistake when you "hear" of crime in Mexico. Chances are that it is crime that took place in Mexico City.

Still a little shaky on the issue of crime in Mexico? Do you need more convincing? Listen to this:

Have you ever visited Los Angeles, Detroit, New York City, or Miami for business or pleasure? Was it a successful and safe trip? Did you walk late at night down dark and unfamiliar streets wearing your most expensive jewelry and flashing huge wads of cash around? Did you visit isolated ATM's alone and in the middle of the night? Did you show off how rich you were at the hotel's bar and then invite the whole lot of them up to you room for a little drinky-poo?

No? This doesn't sound like you at all? You would never do something as stupid as this? You practiced good sense while visiting some of America's most notoriously dangerous cities and lived to tell about it. You had a safe and enjoyable trip and would do it again.

Then, when in Mexico, practice the same good, common sense. Do not do idiotic things that you would never dream of doing while in the dangerous cities in America and you will be a-ok! It is just that simple. Don't be a ding-a-ling and you will do just fine!

In the heartland of Mexico, where we live, it is relatively safe. What little crime we have here (mainly theft) is nothing by comparison to what you will find in Mexico City. My wife can walk unescorted, unmolested, back and forth without a problem. Would she do it carelessly, like at

3:00 a.m. in the morning? Of course not! I wouldn't do it at that hour and I am trained in martial arts. I am talking about exercising good sense no matter where you live.

Crime in Mexico City is a grave problem. We know of Mexicans who left Mexico City because of the crime problem. In fact, the largest increase in crime in Mexico is centered in its capital--Mexico City. It is a city where "pickpockets" were once the major worry. Now, it has evolved into robbery with ice picks, screwdrivers, and even guns.

Other serious crimes are kidnapping and robbery in hijacked taxicabs. This is called *Express Kidnapping*. This involves well-organized professional criminal gangs. These cutthroats normally target the rich members of Mexico's society and, on rare occasions, foreigners.

Their methods remind us of the American carjacker's tactics. What happens is that you get into a stolen cab or a car made to look like a legitimate cab. The driver, one of the gang members, acts like everything is fine and continues to your requested destination. What you don't know is the car that is directly behind you is full of the bogus cabdriver's cohorts.

Your driver suddenly fakes engine failure, signaling his bad-guy pals to close the trap. Someone will spring into your cab with a weapon of some kind, threaten you, scream murderously at you, and perhaps even beat the snot out of you and leave you in a bloodied heap and peso-less. If you are lucky, you will survive the horror.

If you are a person of means, and the criminals know it, they may hold you for a ransom. Be sure to "dress down" and wear no jewelry at all! In the summer of 2004, we heard of a female doctor in Mexico City who had been kidnapped and murdered because her family didn't pay the ransom fast enough. The moral of this story is do not hail cabs from the street. Have your hotel call one for you or go to a cabstand to find one. In addition, make sure you find out the license number of the cab the company is sending to pick you up and only get into that cab. Watch out for these predators in Mexico City!

The breakdown in law and order has resulted in assaults, bank robberies, carjacking, taxi jacking, and kidnapping. It terrifies Mexican citizens trying to get across town.

A prominent columnist, TV personality, and one of Mexico's leading political analysts, Sergio Sarmineto, was kidnapped once and held up twice in a three-year period (Goodness! You would have thought the kidnapping would have taught him to be more careful).

Five men surrounded his car at a stoplight, took him hostage, and kept him in the trunk of his car for two days. They demanded a $50,000.00 ransom that his family luckily paid on time. He was released unharmed — *physically.*

So, terrified of the Mexican City streets, many wealthy citizens (the primary kidnapping targets) are buying protection. They are hiring bodyguards and buying armored cars.

This has created a huge security business in Mexico City, These armored cars, at $50,000 apiece, are selling "hand over fist". One company reports increases of 400% over a three-year period. There are over twenty armored car companies in Mexico City. Anyone who is anybody in the armored car business in the *world* has a plant in Mexico City.

This, of course, leads to the need for professional armored car drivers. There is now a thriving armored car driver training business. But, with almost 16 million violent assaults a year on its citizens, the city should be denied nothing to help combat this war.

Mexico City's crime affects mostly nationals and sometimes foreigners. The U.S. State Department warns against hailing cabs from the street and taking great care when using ATM's.

There are some who would contend though there is a growing problem with crime; the international media are "alarmist, without the vision of a global context". I am not sure what that means. However, when more than half of a city's population is assaulted each year, it sounds bad to me!

Theories abound about the reasons for the breakdown of law and order in Mexico City. It seems silly to me to spend much time trying to figure out the *why* of such a crisis, when they could better spend the energy and resources on figuring out the *how* of fixing the problem. Everyone already knows the crime problem is intolerably bad, so why not come up with a solution rather than more theories? Politicians are the same everywhere, I suppose.

Here are some of the theories:

- Some blame the drug lords for this environment of lawlessness that has infected all of Mexico. However, if this were true, then why isn't there the same degree of crime and violence all over Mexico? You do not *yet* see Mexico City's crime rate reproduced all over Mexico. Some say it is a matter of time. I hope not!

- The socialists (wouldn't you have guessed this one?) blame the disparity between the rich and the poor. That one is so laughable and is an old, old argument. Is it not an excuse for bad behavioral choices? I grew up dirt-poor and never once did I rape, plunder, pillage, or commit general nasty mayhem to take from someone else what didn't belong to me. Nor was I ever tempted to do so!

- A more believable theory is the one that compares the Mexico City problem with Russia and the breakdown of a one-party rule. Though it has led to more freedoms, it has also, just as with the Russians, led to a breakdown in law and order. If you commit a crime in Mexico City, there is a 97% chance you will get away with it. If they catch you, you have only a 3% chance of a conviction! I find this theory more believable.

It is time to dispense with the silly theories and start kicking butts and taking names.

Having pontificated all of that, I must make a sheepish confession: Neither my wife nor I have ever been to Mexico City. And I say this with mixed feelings. On one hand, I feel prudent while on the other, I am a little ashamed.

Here is the deal: We have many Mexican friends here in Guanajuato who would not step one foot in Mexico City for fear of becoming a crime statistic. They are doctors and lawyers who will not, under any circumstance, visit Mexico City. One, whose parents still live there and refuse to move, will fly his folks to Guanajuato, but he will not go there to visit them! Does this speak to you as it does to me? The nationals, at least many of them, fear for their lives in Mexico City.

We have other friends, mostly gringos, who will go to Mexico City routinely, have a gay old time, and return with nary a bit of trouble. One of them, a German expat, conducts tours of the city in English. Go figure!

Who to trust more--The Mexican friends or the others who go to Mexico City often? I don't know. Is it better to err on the side of paranoid caution? For now--you bet!

When Mexico nationals are too afraid to go to Mexico City it causes me to sit up and take notice. And when more than half of Mexico City's citizens are violently assaulted each year--call me an alarmist, but that screams "Red Alert" in my head!

Chapter Four
Can I Afford It?

So, where are we? You know that my wife and I chose Mexico for affordable medical costs, a great climate for better symptom control of my chronic illness, and for the safe environment. But could we afford it? What was the cost of living like? Could we pay the rent and buy food? What about paying for utilities? If the cost of living wasn't within our financial means, then the cheap medical care, the weather, and the safe environment would have done us no good at all.

Trying to discuss the cost of living in Mexico, just like in the United States, can be a confusing, frustrating, and even dizzying experience. This is because cost of living is dependent on location, what the local market will bear, and lifestyle choices.

In the area where my sister lives in North Kansas City, Missouri, for example, housing costs are about half what they are in the Kansas City, Kansas, suburb where my wife and I lived. Location makes all the difference. It is the same in Mexico.

In the central Mexican city of Guanajuato, we live comfortably on around $900 USD a month. If we had chosen Mexico City, Guadalajara, the Lake Chapala area, or even the neighboring city of San Miguel de Allende, we might have more trouble living on this amount.

The deal is the average Mexican family of four exists on about $400 USD a month. They live in a modest home and if they have a car, it is used. They rely heavily on public transportation. They vacation, though not in the pricey resort areas. They go to the doctor when they are ill and they put braces on their children's teeth. The children attend public schools and may even attend the university. They can do all this because not only the cost of living is low here but also because they live frugal lifestyles compared to their U.S. counterparts. Lifestyle choice is the key when trying to assess your projected cost of living in Mexico.

Our cost of living decreased when we moved to Mexico mainly because we made the choice to live, as much as we were able, like a middle-class Mexican family. For example, we try to eat out only once a week. You can do this cheaply by taking advantage of the set meal-of-the-day. The meal includes satisfying portions of a soup, rice or pasta, a main dish, a salad or vegetable and sometimes a drink and dessert for around $4.00 USD.

To save money on groceries, we shop mainly in the neighborhood markets instead of the supermarket, which is more expensive. Shopping like the locals means visiting many shops to buy what one needs rather than going to one store that carries everything. This is more time-consuming, but the quality of the food and the prices are better.

Another way we save money is by using Mexican brands instead of brands imported from the United States. Mexican brands are just as good as U.S. brands (they are often better) and cost less since there is an import tax added to the price of the U.S. brands. Learn to go native and you will find that you can live well for an incredibly small amount of money.

We estimate that our cost of living is about 50% less than it was in the United States. But, remember that lifestyle choice is the key. If you want your SUV; fancy cars; five-bedroom, three-bath house; big-screen TV; satellite dish; expensive vacations or goods imported from the United States, then you may not be able to live for 50% less in Mexico.

Allow me to repeat: It is all but useless to try to predict with any degree of accuracy what your cost of living will be in Mexico. Your lifestyle choices will ultimately determine your cost of living.

Having said that, I realize you need some guidelines to give you some idea of costs. Remember that location is everything. What I will show you are examples of our costs here in Guanajuato.

• Housing--In the heartland, expect to pay about 50% less than you are paying in the United States. Landlords furnish most of the rental apartments and houses right down to the sheets in the bedroom, the towels in the bathroom and dishes, silverware, pots and pans in the kitchen. We rent a small, furnished 2-bedroom, one-bath house complete with telephone, cable TV hook-up, patio, and washing machine for 4500 pesos a month (at the current exchange rate that is about $400 USD). We live on a private street in an expensive area of town. Many locations are just as lovely (if not as quiet as our area) where one can find rentals from around $200-300 USD a month.

- Electricity--Your electric bill will be reasonably cheap (we pay less than $30.00 USD a month) since you will not have air-conditioning or central heating. Also, your water heater and stove will likely be gas. Our electric bill was higher than normal in January because we had to use a space heater in the mornings and evenings when the lows dropped into the 40's.
- Water--Your tap water will be around $15.00 USD a month. It will be higher if you have a washing machine. If you take numerous showers or filter your tap water to drink, expect to pay more than $15.00.
- Bottled water--Your drinking and cooking water will be about $15.00 USD a month (for two people). Bottled water comes in 5-gallon jugs and costs $18 pesos (about $1.60 USD). Before switching to a water filter, the two of us were using between two and three bottles a week.
- Gas--Your water heater and stove will probably use gas rather than electricity. Clothes dryers are not common, but if you have one, it may be gas. Since you probably will not have central heat in your house or apartment, your gas bill will be low. Gas usually comes in tanks that cost about $225 pesos (about $20.00 USD) each. For us, a tank lasts between 4 and 6 weeks.
- Telephone--Basic telephone service is $20.00 USD a month. Be advised that this gives you 100 calls each month. If you have a dial-up internet connection, be careful to record how many connections you make...each call over 100 costs $1.60 pesos, which can add up fast. Long-distance calls are expensive, especially if you call the United States. Check with your local telephone company to see if they have calling plans that give you a

cheaper rate.

- Internet--There are various Internet providers in Mexico if you have a home computer and want an Internet connection. We have a dial-up service that costs about $17.00 USD a month. Prodigy offers high-speed, broadband connection for around $40.00 USD a month, but is not available in all areas. America Online is also available in some parts of Mexico, though we don't have it in Guanajuato yet. If you don't have a home computer (most Mexicans do not), most towns have numerous Internet cafes that charge from $0.80 to $1.50 USD an hour to use their computers.
- Laundry--This can be a hassle if your house or apartment does not come equipped with a washing machine. Most houses and apartments have a laundry sink, affectionately called the "Mexican Maytag", where you can scrub your clothes by hand. We had one in our first apartment and we never did get the hang of rinsing or wringing. If you have a maid, she will be able to wash your clothes for you (and you will be amazed at how clean your clothes are and how quickly she can get the job done!). If you don't have a laundry sink, your maid will take your dirty clothes to her house to wash and then bring them back (ironed!) the next day. Another choice is to take your clothes to a laundromat. These are professional services that wash and dry your clothes for around $0.35 USD a pound.
- Maid service--Although you may be uncomfortable at the thought of having a maid, let me assure you that virtually everyone in Mexico (except for the very poor) has a maid. This is an honorable profession in Mexico and is inexpensive. The going rate is about $3.00 USD an hour (can you believe it?).

- Other Expenses--Haircuts will cost about $4.00 USD. Other personal items: clothes, shoes, toiletries, and entertainment will depend on your personal habits.
- Medical Costs--A doctor's office call will cost about $15.00 USD for a general practioner and twice that for a specialist. If you see at doctor at the Red Cross, it will cost around $5.50 USD. This is amazing--almost beyond belief. In the 1980s, when my wife and I were newly married, she became ill and had to see a neurologist. Even *then*, this specialist charged $115.00 USD for each office call!

Prescription drugs, which were the primary concern for us, are inexpensive. For a month's supply of Prozac (generic) I pay, out-of-pocket, less than $16.00 USD. A friend of ours who has a serious skin ailment paid $115.00 USD for each tube of a prescription ointment in the USA. Now that she is an expat to Guanajuato, she pays less than $15.00 for each tube and it is the same medicine! I get all my medications for about what I would pay for the co-pay for one medication in the United States. This is incredible!

You will find that most of the drugs you take in the USA have Mexican equivalents that are far less expensive. The newest, just-out-of-the-Research-and-Development-chute drugs will not be. You will have to wait for them to make their Mexican debut. Some medications are imported from the United States and are more expensive in Mexico since there is an import tax.

- Dental Care--Depending on which dentist you see, you will pay anywhere from $50.00 to $80.00 USD for a cleaning. Other dental procedures are significantly less expensive than in the United States.
- Medical Insurance--This is another one of those items that is hard to pin down. This will depend on your age, smoking status, and pre-existing conditions. A Mexican

alternative is the Mexican Social Security Insurance (IMSS). As a legal resident of Mexico, you will be eligible to apply. For a reasonable premium of about $250.00 USD a year, you can get medical, dental, vision, and prescription coverage. We recommend this alternative.

Some of our expat friends have kept medical insurance from the United States. They report to us they've had nothing but trouble in trying to receive reimbursements. What you usually must do is pay out-of-pocket and then seek reimbursement.

If you are on Medicare, the bad news is doctors and hospitals do not accept it for payment. There has been "talk" of pushing it through Congress but up to now-- tough luck!

Other Considerations--A subject not covered in almost all the "How to Expatriate" books is what exactly to do with all your stuff left behind in America. You know what I am talking about. All the personal items (junk?) you have been collecting all of your earthly existence in America. What in God's name are you going to do with it? Store it, sell it, or bring it all with you--just what can you do with it all?

The expats with whom we've spoken are divided into three camps. One is that they will store their stuff with family, friends, and even in commercial storage lockers. It must be nice to have the money to do that!

The second group will go through the heart attack of shipping everything, down to the coasters on the coffee table, because they can't bear to part with their "stuff". You can do this.

The third version, which is what we did, is to sell *everything*, lock, stock, and barrel and buy all new stuff when you move to Mexico.

The biggest problem with alternatives one and two is

that these will substantially increase initial and continuing costs.

Don't forget, the numbers I have quoted so far apply to where we live in the heartland of Mexico--Guanajuato. The prices could be cheaper or inflated beyond your means, depending on location.

There are several little cities not too far from us that are less expensive to live than even Guanajuato. We may one day have a look at these alternatives.

According to the Mercer Human Resource Consulting Cost of living survey 2002, Mexico City ranked as the 28th most expensive city in the world...Los Angeles, Chicago, and San Francisco ranked 19, 20, and 21, respectively. In 2001, Mexico City was number 37.[1]

In Mexico City, depending on which neighborhood you choose, your rent could be as low as $800.00 USD a month to as high as $6,000.00 USD.

So, depending on which city you choose for expatriation, there can be a wide range of prices for Housing, Food, Education, Transportation, Clothing, Recreation, Health, Furniture and Appliances, and Personal Care. Resort areas like Puerto Vallarta with its high cost of living prices will make your head spin like Linda Blair's did in the movie *The Exorcist!*

If you are willing to live in a traditional Mexican town, which means you will have to learn Spanish, you can make out like a bandit. If you want the comfort of living in a gringo-infiltrated community where almost everyone speaks English, then it will cost you. The prices will be artificially inflated because of the gringo community. But, if you can afford it, then knock yourself out. It is your choice.

---

[1](http://www.imercer.com/International/home/Cost_of_living_ran kings.asp).

Chapter Five
Baby Steps

You too have considered moving to Mexico? However, you haven't a clue how to begin. What should you do? What is your first step?

The first step, and we cannot stress this enough, is to be sure you have wrestled with the issue that *Mexico is Not America*! You are deciding to come to a country with a vastly different language, culture, and worldview. If you want to get over culture shock *before* coming here, you have to read everything you can get your hands on about the cultural differences.

My wife and I are still waiting for culture shock to hit us and we've been here since August 1, 2003. We are convinced that, were it not for our preliminary research plus our commitment to learning Spanish *before* moving here, we would have been knee-deep in culture shock our first month. But, we prepared ourselves for the culture before we moved.

The second step you need to take is to grab a pen and a notebook and make a list of your living needs. On the left-hand side, list all your needs for a comfortable life. I am talking about the minimum needs that you don't think you could live without. After you make your list, prioritize the items. This will accomplish two goals.

First, it will jar you to your senses. If you have items on your list like central heat and air-conditioning, screens on every window, reliable postal service, or a place where everyone speaks English, then expatriation to Mexico may not be for you.

Second, it will aid you in deciding just what region of Mexico is right for you. If cost of living is an issue for you, then you might want to consider a non-tourist town like Guanajuato rather than an expensive resort area like Puerto Vallarta. If you feel that you need the support of a large English-speaking community, then San Miguel de Allende or the Lake Chapala area might be your cup of tea.

Remember our reasons for moving to Mexico? Our list included affordable medical care, affordable cost of living, and a climate in which my Fibromyalgia symptoms would improve. Our list also included good public transportation, low crime, and a safe environment.

What climate are you seeking? Will small neighborhood stores satisfy your shopping needs or will nothing less than a Wal-Mart SuperCenter do? Do you want to live in a large city or a small town? Do you speak and understand Spanish or are you willing to learn it? These questions will help you discover the best area for your new home.

The third step you need to take is to Read, Read, and Read! Read everything you can find on the regions of Mexico you are considering. Go to your local public library and read all the guidebooks they have. We found many books about Mexico in our local library, but most were outdated. We chose two or three that we thought were the best and then bought the current versions at a bookstore. That way, we did not have to spend much money buying every guidebook.

Another place for research is the Internet (you knew I would get around to mentioning it, didn't you?). The World Wide Web will not only give you many first-person accounts by expatriates living in the regions you are considering, but will also give you pictures of the cities. Another advantage is that you can join discussion groups and chat rooms where the members are expatriates and live in the areas you are considering. We were able to get many contacts in this manner and received a huge amount of help. In addition, there are several online newsletters that focus on various areas of Mexico that are super-helpful.

The fourth step, once you feel that you have done a comfortable amount of research, is to plan a fact-finding mission to the region you are considering. If you are considering several regions, try to visit them all. Take your time and don't rush this step.

There are all sorts of ways to do this. If you are not limited by financial or time considerations and you love adventure, then striking out on your own and traveling by bus might be the way to go. This assumes that you have a decent command of Spanish and are able to ask for help in finding hotels, restaurants, the bus stations, and the bus schedules.

If your Spanish isn't good, you could do what we did. A creative and fun way to research a particular city or region is to enroll in a language school and stay with a host family.

In February 2003, we enrolled in one of the language schools in Guanajuato. Our host family turned out to be a wonderful couple who were our age. They took us into their home and lives as though we were long-lost relatives. Moving in with a Mexican family and watching how they live will alter your misconceptions about Mexicans and their country.

Living with a Mexican family will give you a new perspective beyond what you can possibly imagine. Living with a family rather than in a hotel will give you people with whom to practice your Spanish lessons. It will also give you a support network to help you in your adjustment to the culture. Most importantly, it will help you decide if living in Mexico is right for you.

We believe that living with a host family and attending a language school on your fact-finding mission will benefit you for the following reasons:

1) It will give you a clear picture of what Mexican living is like in the region you are considering for expatriation.

2) It will greatly reduce the stress of the unknown by providing someone to take care of you (your support network).

3) The host family will provide all your meals. You won't have to worry about finding a restaurant for every meal.

4) You will have someone to answer all your questions, get you out of jams, and genuine experts on the local economy, available rentals, medical care, the best stores, and the best neighborhoods.

5) It will provide you with a local contact should you decide to expatriate to that city or region.

6) The staff at the language school will be a gold mine of information about the city, the region, the history, and the culture.

7) The language schools often plan outings and cultural events for the students so you may be able to travel around the area with a guide and attend cultural events you might

miss if you were on your own.

The fifth step is to make a realistic plan. Let's say that you have finished your fact-finding mission or missions and have decided that a certain city is for you. What is your next step? A plan to return!

After our February 2003 fact-finding trip to Guanajuato, we sat down and made a six-month plan to return for good. This is the most crucial and frightening step of the whole process. What you are doing is planning on how to wrap up your life in the country of your birth and begin a new life in a foreign country.

Here are some considerations:

1) Plan a target return date to your city of choice.

2) Secure your housing. If you did not find housing or make contacts with real estate agents during your fact-finding trip, then check the Internet for listings in the area you have chosen. Also, if you stayed with a host family, ask them if they will keep their eyes open for rentals or houses for sale for you.

3) Decide whether you want to keep all your household goods, keep part of them, store them, move all of them or sell them. We decided to sell most of our possessions and used an estate sale broker to carry it out. We brought some clothes, toiletries, and a few books with us on the airplane. We mailed some items to our new address before we left, and stored a few items with family. Some expatriates bring the contents of their houses to Mexico with them. Others sell everything and buy new household goods here.

4) Visa considerations: If you have decided that you want to come to Mexico for six months or a year to try it out, then all you need is a tourist visa. If you enter the country by plane, the cost of the visa will be included in the airfare. The steward or stewardess will give you the necessary form that you will give to the immigration official in the

airport after you land. If you cross the border by car or bus, you will have to stop at the immigration office, fill out the necessary forms, and pay a fee (about $20 USD).

Most customs officials will ask you how long you plan to stay in the country. Most will give you 180 days if you ask for that many. However, the customs officials know all about the Ugly American Syndrome. These people come into Mexico demanding all manner of considerations. The customs officer is just liable to give you a thirty-day visa, no matter how hard you beg. The actions and attitudes from previous Americans affect his or her attitude. This happens most often in Mexico City airport, but prepare for it no matter what entry point you use.

When we have used the bus to make trips to the U.S.A., on our return, the customs officers have always asked us how long we plan to stay in the country. We have always said we wanted 180 days and that is what we've always been given.

Don't worry if you are only issued a 30-day visa and you plan to stay longer. You will need to go to the nearest immigration office within that 30-day period and apply for an extension. It's not difficult, but it can be a hassle if the nearest immigration office is some distance away from the city you are visiting. If you want to stay longer than 180 days, you will have to cross the border back into the U.S.A. and then come back into Mexico. There is some talk that Mexico will restrict the number of times a person can receive a tourist visa, but it hasn't happened yet. In fact, we know people who have lived in Mexico for many years on tourist visas. They just have to make trips back to the U.S.A. every 180 days.

If you are planning to stay in Mexico for more than a year, then you can apply for an FM-3 (resident) visa. You can do this at a Mexican embassy in the U.S.A. You can also apply for it at a Mexican immigration office once you arrive in Mexico.

This visa requires more paperwork than a tourist visa, which is why we recommend a private service to help you with the application. These people do everything short of standing in for the required photos and fingerprints. For a fee, they will fill out all the necessary forms and photocopy all the required documents. They will stand in line at the bank to pay the various fees and go to the American embassy to get a letter confirming your financial solvency.

We have heard many stories of frustration from other expatriates who try to complete the application without help. Some had to return to the immigration office five or six times before the officials finally had all the necessary paperwork! On the other hand, we've heard from other expatriates who breezed through the application without any trouble. For us, paying the fee for the private service was worth it to avoid potential hassles.

The FM-3 visa is renewable once a year, but does not require a trip to the U.S.A. like a tourist visa. The FM-3 visa allows you to come and go across the border as many times as you please. It does not change your U.S. citizenship, just your place of residency.

The requirements for getting an FM-3 are as follows:
1) Bank statements from the three months before your application showing an income of $1,000 USD for the primary applicant and $500 USD for each dependent.
2) A letter stating why you want an FM-3. The private services will write the letter for you after asking for your reasons.
3) Your tourist visa and copies of every page of your passport, even the blank pages.
4) Some offices require a copy of your marriage license, if applicable.

5) Passport photos of all applicants. These must be a certain size and must show both full-face and side views. If you use a private service, they will take the photos so you will have exactly what the immigration office requires.

6) The immigration office will give you several forms that you must fill out. Again, the private service will do this for you after you provide them with the necessary information.

There are several types of FM-3 visas. If you are planning on working in Mexico, you will need a specific visa. Your employer should help you to get this visa. If you are planning to be a full-time student, you will need a different visa. Your school should be able to help you with the application.

The sixth step is to work your plan. Break down your plan to expatriate into workable and flexible steps. Set target dates for each step. This will help keep the plan from seeming too overwhelming.

The seventh step is to take a deep breath and make the move! Get on that plane, bus, or car and start your new life in Mexico.

Some last minute considerations include:

Don't forget to deal with your mail. The mail service in Mexico is not the best, so don't plan to have the U.S. Postal Service forward it to your new Mexican address. Chances are it will never arrive. You can rent a post office box in the U.S. and ask a trusted friend or family member to send your mail to you periodically via UPS or DHL. You can also rent a mailbox through a private service, like Mailbox, Etc., which has branches in Mexico.

Make sure your lawyer knows your new address if you have legal concerns.

Chapter Six
Setting Up House

Water

A favorite story, told to me by a close friend on hearing our plans to move to Mexico, was that we would get bloody amoebic dysentery from the water and die.

I would like to announce that we are very much alive and have not died because of living in Mexico.

It seems the mere mention of Mexican water evokes the most emotional responses from Americans. Everyone has a Mexican water story. Have you ever been in a social gathering when someone mentions that so-and-so is planning to vacation in Mexico? The whole room erupts into statements like, "I hope they remember not to drink the water!"

The problem with these rumors and half-truths is that you never hear of the thousands of tourists who visit Mexico each year and *never* get sick. What you do hear about are the few who do become ill.

I am not convinced that it is the water that makes tourists ill. Rather, I think a food-borne bacterium is what makes people (including Mexicans) ill. Tourists will recklessly "eat off the streets" from food vendors (more on that subject later). I think this unwise practice is the main cause of the "turista" illness and not something in the water.

Tap water is *not* safe to drink in Mexico. However, the water in the tourist resorts supposedly is safe, but ask the hotel staff to be sure. One sip is not enough to make you ill. Constantly challenging your body's immune system by *always* drinking tap water can make you ill.

We've heard many reasons about why the water is unsafe, but have not been able to confirm the cause. One reason people gives is the infrastructure of the cities is old and the pipes that carry the water decay over time, allowing contamination to seep into the water. Another is the population has grown too much for the water treatment plants to be able to treat the water effectively. During the rainy season, there is so much rainwater the water treatment plants cannot deal with the volume of water that flows through the system.

So, what does one do for drinking water in the home? There are a few choices available. One is to get your drinking and cooking water from a company that sells purified water in five-gallon jugs. In most areas, the water will be delivered to your door (and into your kitchen if you ask) for about $18 pesos for each jug. There are dispensers that you can use if you have the strength to hoist the heavy jugs upside down into them. Otherwise, there are siphons that pump the water out of the jug, making it unnecessary to lift the jugs off the floor.

Another alternative is to use a water filter. There are single-faucet filters and whole-house filters. We have one attached to the faucet in the kitchen that filters out 99.9% of the bacteria as well as the sediment that gets into the pipes.

I highly recommend this choice! I quickly became tired of having to hoist those insanely heavy five-gallon jugs of water! It was breaking my back. Therefore, we got a water filter. Buy one *before* coming to Mexico and bring it with you! It is well worth the time and effort to do so, in my view!

Some people purify their water with iodine or chlorine drops, available at most food stores and pharmacies.

A final alternative is to boil water for drinking, though we've found there are several opinions about how long to let the water boil to purify it—ranging from 10 minutes to 40 minutes. We, personally, don't use this option because we have very hard water in Guanajuato and don't like the way the water tastes.

Don't worry about using tap water to brush your teeth or for bathing. Chances are you will never get sick. I've brushed my teeth with tap water the whole time we've lived in Mexico and have never suffered any ill effects. My wife, on the other hand, always uses filtered water to brush her teeth. Just be careful not to swallow the water and you should be fine.

If you do contract "La Turista", don't panic and don't blame the water. It was more than likely something you ate. Go to a clinic or a pharmacy and they will fix you right up. Even Mexicans get "La Turista" occasionally, so doctors and pharmacists are knowledgeable in how to treat it.

Grocery Shopping

You can live in Mexico for much less money than you did in the United States if you shop like a native. In this section, we hope to tell you how to save money on your grocery bill.

Shopping for food in Mexico is almost a daily affair. It can also be quite adventurous. Now, shopping is not one of my favorite activities (I'm a guy--what do you expect!). It is strictly my wife's domain (and she's not all that fond of it either!), but I do often tag along because it can be an interesting outing.

My observation has been that daily shopping is much more than the mere "hunting and gathering" of the family's daily bread (or tortillas). It is a huge social affair where neighbors meet with one other, exchange gossip and, incidentally, shop for food. There are huge markets, both open-air and in enclosed buildings, and small neighborhood grocery stores (some no bigger than a good-sized walk-in closet).

Open-air markets are an ancient tradition stemming from before the Spanish invasion. They are a common sight in all of Mexico. They are similar to the farmer's markets in America, but more eclectic in their scope. They have a wide variety of foods (and many other items) to delight the eye, tempt the palate, and prices to please your wallet.

In these markets, you can buy fruits and vegetables grown using time-honored farming traditions that increase the taste. Many fruits and vegetables are native to Mexico that you are unlikely to find in your U.S. supermarket.

Farmers grow the produce for the local market. Therefore, they pick it when it is ripe instead of picking it much too early to survive shipping to a distant market.

This radically affects the taste. You will find the produce has a richer taste than what you are accustomed to finding in your supermarket produce section.

Our neighborhood's open-air market has stalls that are open every day, but it doesn't get into full swing until the weekend. It contains four warehouse-type buildings, around which dozens of booths spring up for the weekend. The booths consist of large tables, piled high with a variety of goods, and shaded by a tarp strung overhead. Some booths sell just one item--jeans, shoes, t-shirts, or electrical appliances. Some sell a wide variety of items. You might find a vendor selling candy, toiletries, movies, kitchen items and baby clothes--all piled on one table.

You can find just about anything you need in one of these markets. There are butcher shops and seafood stands. There are tiny grocery stores selling canned goods, laundry detergent, milk, cheese, and eggs. You will find fruit and vegetable stands, tiny hardware shops, and people selling pet supplies. People sell CDs, movies, clothes, and much more. Interspersed among the booths are many lunch counters where you can eat a meal or a snack.

Now, we must deal with buying meat. If you don't know what to expect, this could chill you to the bone and may turn you into a vegetarian.

If you are up early to get a head start on your shopping, you might just have the delightful experience of seeing a local rancher pull up to the neighborhood butcher shop in his old, rickety pickup. In the truck bed, you will see a small mountain of slaughtered pig, goat, sheep, calf, or bull, still sporting hide, hair, feet, and sometimes the head! Needless to say, this sight takes some getting used to. However, it is a common sight.

One of the times we were in the open-air market, my

wife almost was conked in the head by the bloody carcass of some animal that was slung over the shoulder of the deliveryman. Attached to this hunk of whatever was a large, soccer-ball-sized organ that was a sickening shade of gray. It was bouncing with the man's every step and was making a squashy sound like gelatin does when you shake it. Isn't that gross?

For those of us who are faint-of-heart and feeling a bit queasy about now, there is an alternative to buying your meat at the local butcher shop. If you want your meat neatly packaged with nary a hint of its origins, you can shop at a supermarket instead. Supermarkets in Mexico are much like the ones in the U.S.A. but the prices are higher than you will find in the neighborhood shops and markets. Go native and patronize the neighborhood stores and markets where the locals shop and you will save money.

A word of warning--I draw the line at going native when it comes to pickled chicken feet, pig feet, pig ears, and pig snout! You probably think that only a few people eat these, but they are considered a delicacy. You can see people everywhere in Guanajuato chomping down on these items.

I love Mexico and everything Mexican...well, almost everything. However, the sight of gallon jars holding an assortment of pig extremities or chicken feet floating in a noxious-looking, cloudy liquid is something I cannot love! You can find jars of pinkish-gray, swollen, jelly-like delicacies in every market, including the supermarket.

If you find this a bit sickening, read on! We've watched people eat these yummy tidbits with a great deal of enthusiasm. One older lady slapped a nice-sized piece of pig snout into a tortilla, covered it with a generous serving of salsa, bit into it, and rolled her eyes in delight.

This gets worse. You can buy an entire pig head if you wish. One day, we were scanning the supermarket's flyer to see what was on sale before beginning our shopping. In the flyer's meat section, we saw a picture of a pig head. Not quite believing our eyes, we walked immediately to the meat case. There, taking center stage was a pig's head. Not only was it an entire head, the butcher had formed its mouth into a smile!

We still don't know if people buy the complete head, take it home and cook it up for a family get-together or just ask the butcher to slice off a few pieces. And what do you ask for? Do you ask for a couple of slices of ear and a hunk of cheek? A piece of snout and some jowl? Which part is the best? I can't get the image of the pig's head out of my mind...I think I'm suffering from post-traumatic pig head syndrome!

You can find people cooking another delicacy in the market, along a street or outside someone's front door. It is something that smells so good it makes your mouth water. You just have to find the source of the smell and eat whatever it is. That is, until you get a glimpse of what is cooking. In the wok-like skillet are little pieces of what looks like gray tubular pasta. Only they aren't pieces of pasta—they are intestines!

On a final note, there are even stores where one can go buy entrails. I am not joking! There is a store in our neighborhood with a hand-lettered sign next to the door that says: Entrails, heart, liver, tongue, tripe, intestines, and head! They also sell menudo, which is a very spicy soup with various entrails in it. Supposedly, menudo is the cure of choice for a hangover--either the spice makes you sweat the alcohol out of your body or the sight of entrails in your bowl makes you throw up. I'm not sure which.

Finding Housing

Whatever region of Mexico strikes your fancy, an excellent piece of advice about housing is to rent first, buy later.

The first reason is, if you rent first, you can try out several regions of Mexico before deciding which one is right for you. Also, if you rent first, you can try out several, or all, of the various barrios (neighborhoods) in the city you choose.

The second reason is that home ownership, no matter the country, can be a money pit. Also, unless your Spanish is *very* good, you could have difficulty dealing with the various people necessary to help you in finding and buying a house. Also, you could have difficulty communicating with any contractors and workers you hire if the house needs repairs or remodeling. If you cannot communicate well, how will you know if your real estate agent is honest? How will you tell your contractor what work is necessary and when you expect him to finish the work? How will you settle disputes? These are not impossible to overcome, but they are worth considering.

Other ways to find housing include checking the classified ads in the local newspapers, looking for bulletin boards in markets, coffee shops, Internet cafes, and around the universities. Another good idea is to walk around various neighborhoods to get a "feel" for the area. Look for signs posted in windows and on doors. You can also ask shop owners and people on the street in the neighborhood you like if they know of any rentals or houses for sale. Many people find housing by word-of-mouth. You may find a place that has just become available, or will be shortly, which the owner hasn't advertised yet.

If your Spanish is not that good, look in the telephone

yellow pages for language schools. Note the ads for schools that offer English classes. Go to the school and introduce yourself. Ask if you could hire one of their advanced English students to act as your interpreter in your search to find housing. Be sure to pay this person well for his or her time. Many of these are struggling university students who are busy and need extra money.

In the regions where gringos congregate--Guadalajara, the Lake Chapala area, Puerto Vallarta, and San Miguel de Allende--you will find that many people speak English. In fact, many Mexicans speak at least a little English. In other areas, like Guanajuato, it may be difficult to find many people who speak English other than expatriates.

Once you have mastered house hunting in Mexico and have found some potential places to hang your hat, there are some items you need to examine. Here is a helpful checklist to use before you fork over your pesos:

1) Make sure there is a hot water heater. It will probably be on a patio or in the bathroom. Ask the landlord to show you how to light it. The pilot light will go out when your gas tank runs out of gas and your landlord may not be available to light it again. Also, if the hot water heater is located outside, the pilot light may blow out when there is a lot of wind.

Gas usually comes in four-foot-high tanks stored on a patio or terrace. Ask the landlord to show you where they are located and how to switch from one tank to the other. When the pilot light on your water heater won't stay lit or you can't light the burner on your stove, you will know it's time to switch the empty tank to the full one. Some houses and apartments have large gas tanks on the roof. Ask the landlord how to read the gauge on the rooftop tank so you will know when you need to have it filled. Also, ask the landlord who is responsible for calling the gas company and paying for the delivery. We call our landlady when we need gas, she pays the delivery person, and we reimburse her when we pay the rent.

2) Try all the faucets, flush the toilet, and turn on the shower. Make sure there are no leaks, the water is clean, and there is enough water pressure. Also, make sure that all the faucets have hot and cold water—one house we looked at only had cold water in the kitchen!

3) Check to see how many electric outlets there are in each room. Are there enough to meet your needs? Ask the landlord if there are frequent power outages. Ask where the fuse box is located and how to change the fuses. Also, ask if there is sufficient power to run more than one appliance at a time (we cannot use our computer when we use the washing machine). We recommend you use at least a surge protector for your electrical appliances; a voltage regulator with battery backup is recommended if you have a computer, as there are frequent power surges and occasional power outages.

4) Check to see if there is a phone line and a phone in the house. It can take up to two years to get a phone line put in your house, so if a phone is something you need, it is better to find a place that has an existing line. Also, be sure to ask if the previous bill has been paid—if it is unpaid, you will not be able to use the phone.

5) Ask the landlord for an estimate of the cost of utilities. Ask who is responsible to pay the bills. Our landlady pays the bills and then we pay her when we pay the rent. It can be a hassle to go to all the various utility offices and stand in long lines to pay your bills.

6) Ask if there has been a history of bug problems in the house or apartment. Who is responsible for fumigation? In our first apartment, we had a terrible problem with scorpions. Fortunately, we've only seen two scorpions in

our present house.

7) Check to see if you can find evidence of leaks around the windows and ceiling. We have found that windows here usually leak when it rains. Ask who is responsible for repairs if there is a leak in the roof or if there is damage because of leaky windows.

8) Check all window and door locks to make sure they work properly. Also, make sure the bars on the windows are strong and don't need to be repaired.

9) If the house or apartment is furnished, is there furniture to meet your needs? If there is something you need, ask the landlord if he or she has something you can use. Are there enough pots and pans, dishes, silverware, towels, sheets and blankets?

10) Do the bedrooms have closets? Many Mexican homes do not have closets, but there may be wardrobes where you can store your clothes. Ask the landlord to supply a wardrobe or chest of drawers if there isn't a place to put your clothes.

11) Ask the landlord where you can find the nearest market, pharmacy, doctor, dentist, hospital, and laundromat. Ask him for recommendations.

12) Ask whether the trash is picked up or if you need to take it to a dumpster. Ask where you can find the nearest dumpster.

13) Check the area around the house or apartment. Is it located on a busy street or near a school? Is there a bar or cantina nearby? If you want a quiet place in which to live, you will not want to live close to a busy street, bar or school. Is there a bus stop close to the house?

14) How much notice will you need to give before moving out? What happens if you need to move before your lease expires? How long will it take for the landlord to refund any deposits you paid before moving in? Will you lose all

or part of your deposit if you break the lease?

15) Ask if the plumbing lines are vented. If they are not, gas from the sewer will come up out of the drains. You can easily solve this by placing flat, rubber stoppers over all the drains.

16) Be sure to ask if the rent the landlord quotes is in dollars or in pesos.

17) If you improve the property, will your landlord increase the rent as a result? Are you allowed to make any changes?

18) If there is a maid or gardener, who is responsible for paying him or her? Are you able to assign tasks to them? What if his or her work doesn't satisfy you?

Maid Service

Almost everyone in Mexico, except the very poor, has a maid. It is an honorable profession here, so don't feel uncomfortable about having one. The cost is so low that it doesn't make sense not to employ a maid unless you love cleaning the toilet.

Ask your landlord or neighbors who they recommend. Your landlord may employ a full-time maid to clean all his properties, so you won't have to find your own. Often, when expatriates move into a neighborhood, there will be a nonstop stream of women looking for a job. It is safer to get recommendations from your landlord, neighbors, or other expatriates rather than hire someone who comes to your door.

Mexican law heavily favors the rights of employees. If you hire a maid, gardener, or other employee, you will want to check with a lawyer (abogado) to make sure you meet all your legal obligations. Besides paying a decent wage, be sure to treat your employee with large doses of honor and respect.

Some maids will cook you a meal as well as cleaning the house and doing the laundry. If this is part of your agreement, make sure you have all the ingredients she will need for the meal. You may want to specify how hot (picante) you like your food; otherwise she may use more chilies than you can tolerate. Also, be sure she has all the cleaning products and tools she needs. She may hesitate to ask you for certain items, so ask often if there is anything she needs. Ask her which products and brands she prefers and make sure you keep them in stock.

Your Car

If you choose to bring a car into Mexico, what to do with it could pose a problem. For example, in Guanajuato, parking is at an extreme premium. I know an expat here who pays handsomely for parking a monstrous car that he rarely uses. Therefore, keep that in mind.

The house where we live has an enormous driveway and we have chosen to be car-less. We could put four standard-sized SUV's in it, but no one uses it! Perhaps we should rent it out.

Fruits and Vegetables

You *must*, you have no choice, soak your fruits and vegetables here in Mexico, unless you can peel them. Some people say that you don't have to soak them if you are going to cook them, but we do anyway. I know this will impose a boring routine on your schedule that you feel you could live without, but it is a necessity--there is no other choice if you want to live here. You will be able to buy several different products to do this. You can use either chlorine or iodine drops for this task. Most markets carry these products. The labels have directions on their use.

Post Office

The Mexican Postal Service truly lives up to *all* the stereotypes you have no doubt heard. It deserves its bad reputation that is reinforced with each passing day!

It stinks, it's awful, it's horrid, and it's from the Middle Ages! We've had the most horrible time getting mail from the United States. Mail to America usually gets there fine, but good luck in getting something from the United States.

I trust the Post Office here to get something insignificant and of little value to America. However, if I had to mail something of value, like a writing contract to a publisher, I would not trust the Mexican Postal Service. I would send it by some private international courier service. We have DHL and UPS here and they've proven reliable--so far!

Banks

You cannot simply waltz into a bank and open an account. You must have the following documents: passport, FM3 or FM2 Visa, a copy of your rental lease or proof of your home ownership, a copy of a utility bill with the address matching the lease or house title.

Having said all that, I must tell you that not all banks stick to this so-called legal proof of your residency here in Mexico. We went to three banks with the aforementioned documentation and were refused by all three banks! And, I cannot possibly tell you why! They all had these silly stories about the documentation being incomplete or invalid. This is a common response in any Mexican bureaucracy! If they don't want to deal with you, then suddenly all of your papers aren't right--"Come later, please!"

The fourth bank not only opened the account at once, but also told us most of the documentation we brought wasn't necessary at all! This is what you will face if you want to expatriate to Mexico and there is nothing you can do about it.

As you can see, setting up house in this culture can be different from the United States. It takes some patience and fortitude. You have to be able to "roll with the punches" because there are indeed many "punches" with which you will have to roll if you expatriate here.

Chapter Seven
Gringo Landia

According to the 2000 Statistical Yearbook of the Immigration and Naturalization Service, published by the Bureau of Citizenship and Immigration Service, an estimated 300,000 Americans would expatriate to other countries *each year* between 2000 and 2005. Some estimates predict the number will continue to increase each year after 2005. Americans are leaving the country in droves.

A 1999 report, put together by the U.S. Bureau of Consular Affairs, estimated that 748,780 Americans were living in Mexico. No doubt, the amount has increased in the 6 years since the Bureau published the report, but by how much is a guess. Factual statistics of today's numbers are difficult to obtain since many Americans come to Mexico seeking anonymity and therefore want to remain untraceable.

Americans expatriate to Mexico for various reasons. It used to be that retirees were the only population group one could find living in Mexico. Retirement is no longer the primary reason for Americans to expatriate to Mexico. We've met couples with children who have moved to Mexico. We have also met young adults in their 20s and 30s who have settled here.

Reasons for expatriating abound. Some people come for the climate, because of health issues or for economic reasons. Some come to provide a new cultural experience for the children or to learn Spanish. Some expatriate because they can't stand to live in America any longer or are afraid of the threat of terrorism. Many come to find a lower cost of living, to work, to write, to create art, or to get back to real community living. Of course, retirement is still a reason to expatriate.

Mexico attracts expatriates from the U.S.A. because of its low cost of living and proximity to family and friends in the States. You can jump on a plane in Leon, Guanajuato, and be in Houston, Texas, in less than 2 hours. Mexico works for many Americans.

So, you ask, where do all these American expatriates live after their flight from America? Are there any particular regions of Mexico where Americans congregate?

You can find Americans almost anywhere in Mexico. You will find them in Baja California, in the Yucatan, in central Mexico, in Mexico City (though I don't understand why anyone would want to live there), and along the coasts--especially the famous Gold (west) Coast. There are students, teachers, writers, artists, scientists, professors, and retirees.

The densest populations of gringos are in San Miguel de Allende, Guadalajara, the Lake Chapala area, and Mexico's famous west-coast cities--San Carlos Bay, Mazatlan, Puerto

Vallarta, Nuevo Vallarta, Manzanillo, Acapulco, Cabo San Lucas, and Ixtapa.

Guadalajara, for example, has between 20,000 and 25,000 American expatriates and a total population of 6 million. The Lake Chapala area, which has a population of around 80,000, has around 8,000 expatriates. San Miguel de Allende, which has a total population of around 80,000, has between 8,000 and 10,000 expatriates. Puerto Vallarta has a total population of 250,000 and has an estimated expatriate population of 20,000. The rest of the American expatriates migrate all over Mexico.

There is a common thread that explains why so many gringos congregate in the regions that we call "Gringo Land".

Climate is an often-cited reason for living in these popular areas. There is a climate for everyone in Mexico. If you love a mountainous desert-dry climate, then San Miguel de Allende awaits you. If you love the beach, the jungle heat, and humidity, then Mexico's Gold Coast is just the place for you to put down roots.

Good medical care is another attraction. Medical care in "Gringo Land" is good to superior. In the Guadalajara area, there is access to medical schools and hospitals that offer top-notch medical care with up-to-date treatments. There are also a good number of bilingual doctors and medical personnel. Puerto Vallarta has two hospitals and many bilingual medical personnel. It also has some alternative health care choices. In San Miguel de Allende, you will also find bilingual medical personnel and a host of specialists.

These areas offer an abundance of cultural and recreational activities that attract American and Canadian expatriates. There are country clubs, golf courses, tennis courts, swimming pools, and health clubs in all of these locations. Along the coasts, there are a host of water-related sports like fishing, boating, surfing, water-skiing, and sailing. All these cities offer movies (some in English), English-language lending libraries, volunteer opportunities, and concerts. In addition, there are charity fund-raisers for a host of causes-literacy, toys and clothing for orphans, building libraries, scholarships, and to provide free (or low-cost) care for pets.

Some gringos will band together to provide English classes for the locals. I think that is a great idea! Even in our adopted town of Guanajuato, which only has about 150 expatriates, there is some effort to provide free English classes and to raise money for humanitarian causes.

The most common reason that Americans are attracted to the "Gringo Land" regions is there is already an English-speaking gringo community in place. I understand the attraction and the advantages of moving to a region where you can blend in with the existing gringos.

Let's say you are in your early 60s. You have never lived in a foreign country nor studied a foreign language (at least since high school). The idea of great year-round weather, great medical care, and cultural opportunities appeals to you. Let's say that you want to live in a traditional Mexican town where few, if any, of the other residents speak English. However, since you can't speak Spanish, the decision weighs heavily on your mind. It scares you a bit too much to plunge into the thick of everything.

An alternative is to rent a house or apartment in the Lake Chapala area, San Miguel de Allende or one of the other "Gringo Land" regions for a year or two. During this time, you can study Spanish diligently and absorb the culture with the help and support of the large gringo population. Then, when you are comfortable with your language skills, you can move on to a region with fewer English-speakers if you wish. I understand this alternative.

What I don't understand at all is why, in these English-speaking enclaves, they erect *gated communities and form neighborhood associations* with their inevitable political squabbling for positions of power. I also do not understand why they build subdivisions indistinguishable from their American counterparts.

In almost every city that has many gringos, you will find *exclusive gated communities*. Why? They can't be in response to crime because there is little crime in the surrounding area (and, there is research that shows that gated communities do not deter criminals). Just what do these gringo expatriates believe they need to be gated from? What or who are they trying to keep out of their neighborhoods?

Keeping to themselves in their fortress enclaves has two results. First, they isolate themselves from and, therefore, fail to associate with their Mexican neighbors. Second, they don't become fluent in Spanish because they severely limit their opportunities to practice.

I would be rich today if I had a dollar for every time I have heard the following:

"When those Mexicans (or whoever) come to our country, they should have to learn English and live in regular neighborhoods like the rest of us."

In Kansas City, our home before moving to Mexico, there has been a large Hispanic community for decades. In the last three years, the population has increased by almost 300%. Most live in an area called "Little Mexico" with stores and services that cater to the Mexican population. Everyone speaks Spanish. It is much like Chinatown in Los Angeles. Many middle-aged and older people never learn English, though they want their children and grandchildren to be fluent in English and Spanish. Some families move out of "Little Mexico" eventually and integrate with the rest of the population.

Well folks, clearly there is a double standard here. When Mexicans or whoever move to the U.S.A., Americans expect them to learn English pronto. Americans expect them to move out of their ethnic enclaves and integrate into the rest of the population. However, when Americans move to Mexico, they don't require themselves to learn Spanish. They refuse to integrate with the Mexican population and they build gringo enclaves. They may say that anyone can move into the houses in their exclusive fortresses. Well, only a small percentage of Mexican families earn over $60,000 USD a year; therefore, how can these families afford a house that costs several hundred thousand dollars (or more)?

We knew many Mexicans in Kansas City who wanted to learn English, but did not earn enough money in their menial-labor jobs to afford the classes. However, they did what they could to make sure their children had every opportunity to learn English so they would be able to find good jobs. I doubt if the gringos living in these exclusive gated communities can use the excuse of not being able to learn Spanish because they can't afford the classes! What do you think?

While a few gringos *do* learn Spanish and *do* live in Mexican neighborhoods, there are enough who don't to cause some friction between themselves and the native population. We've been told by people who are former residents of "Gringo Land" that most of the residents don't bother to learn any Spanish. In fact, while writing this chapter, we met a lovely couple from the Lake Chapala area who were visiting Guanajuato. They confirmed that *most* of the expatriates in their area refuse to either learn the language or associate with their Mexican neighbors. Again, I have to ask why?

This has both confused and annoyed me for some time. When confused or annoyed, I go into research mode. I ran across something in doing research that offered a possible answer to my question. Note: it is only a *possible* explanation.

The Pacific coast of Mexico as far south as Acapulco and as far north as Mazatlan is teeming with gated communities for gringos and million-dollar homes. This area has been referred to as Mexico's *Gold Coast*.

This is an interesting term with which I was unfamiliar. Having grown up in the poor shmuck class and not the American aristocracy, I had never heard this term until I read a book by best-selling author Nelson DeMille, called *The Gold Coast*. It is a great book and will give you some insight into the mind-set shared by the gringo population in these regions (remember, this is just my take on the situation).

"Gold Coast" was a term used to describe an area of New York's Long Island where residents built colonial-era villages and monolithic estates. It was an area where a lifestyle of exclusivity prevailed. The riffraff and rabble were kept out so as not to taint the lives of the wealthy.

"It is an area of old money, old families, old social graces, and old ideas about who should be allowed to vote, not to mention who should be allowed to own land. The Gold Coast is not a pastoral Jeffersonian democracy."[2]

The huge estates that they built were essentially *gated communities*. It wasn't enough to have massive acreages of land on which to build mansions in the French or Italian

---

[2] The Gold Coast; Nelson DeMille; Warner Books, Inc.; 1990; Page 5

style--the likes of which the common man (peasants) had never seen. These rich people walled in the land, erected fortress-like walls complete with iron gates and gatehouses, and hired live-in gatekeepers to keep out the riffraff.

Am I on the wrong track here? Is not the reason for having these fortresses, gates, and gatekeepers to keep the rabble (the peasants) from bothering the Lords of the Manor? If, for the sake of argument, I am correct in my assumption, then who are the Lords of the Manor behind the gates and walls and who are the riffraff in these *gated communities* in Mexico?

I have seen these *gated communities* in San Miguel de Allende and Puerto Vallarta. The houses are ultra expensive and make me wonder how a middle-class Mexican family could ever begin to afford to buy one. This, of course, leads me to assume that these homes and communities are meant for only a certain *class* of people. They are for the rich Mexican (of which there are very few) and the gloriously rich American and Canadian expatriates.

On Sundays, there is a half-hour infomercial on our local television station that advertises these homes. The narrator used the words "exclusive" and "exclusivity" in every other sentence. They constantly highlight the same amenities which these *gated communities* have in common with Long Island's Gold Coast estates. They have walls surrounding the community, security guards and cameras, and 24/7 gatekeepers who are always at the ready to keep out the "undesirables." Again I ask, just who are these "undesirables?"

Of the Long Island Gold Coast architecture, DeMille says:

"But the architects and their American clients of this period were not looking into the future, or even trying to create the present, they were looking back over their shoulders into a European past that had flowered and died even before the first block of granite arrived on this site. What these people were trying to create or recreate in the New World is beyond me." [3]

I just wonder in which direction the builders of and homebuyers in these gringo-gated communities have been looking. Have they been looking at the future, the present, or looking over their shoulders into an American past? I also wonder what these people are trying to create or recreate on Mexico's Gold Coast and in other regions in this country that has graciously allowed them to live here as guests. It is beyond me.

"I can't put myself in their minds or hearts, but I can sympathize with their struggle for an identity, with their puzzlement, which has troubled Americans from the very beginning--who are we, where do we fit, where are we going?"[4]

Though I don't understand it, perhaps I too can sympathize with the identity struggle behind the erecting of these gated communities and the isolation from the Mexican people they create. The Mexican people genuinely don't understand why these gringos come to Mexico and refuse to socialize or interact with them in any way. We've had Mexicans ask us:

"Why won't these Americans learn Spanish?"

"Why won't these Americans associate with us? What is wrong with us?"

---

[3] Ibid; Page 62
[4] Ibid; Page 62

One cannot learn the language while hiding behind the walls of a fortress and refusing to interact with the Mexican population. The Mexicans are genuinely hurt by this attitude of isolation. They've told us so.

"The whole silly Gold Coast was a sham, an American anomaly, in a country that was an anomaly to the rest of the world." [5]

Sadly, I think the Gringo Land expats display the same sham to the locals in the cities where the gringo enclaves exist. The relationship between the locals and their gringo *guests* is flimsy, at best.

Another issue that has to do with the Americanization of *all* of Mexico, not just the "Gringo Land" cities, is the introduction of American-made products and American television programs.

Let me say from the beginning the issue is not just the mere introduction of American products that may or may not compete with similar Mexican products. It is an issue of the means by which these products are being introduced into Mexico.

If ever a country wanted to change the unique cultural identity of its people by altering their ethical and moral values, the instrument of choice is television. People copy what they see on American television programs and in American television commercials.

I must admit that I have never been fond of American television commercials. I have rarely seen any that I could consider to be clever. This is because being clever and witty doesn't sell products as well as being stupid and inane and having questionable ethics does.

---

[5] (Ibid; Page 63).

America is slowly and surely beginning to weave its own unique brand of morality into the fabric of Mexican society through American-produced commercials and programs. It is doing in Mexico what has been done in America in the past few decades. It appears the same themes of civil disobedience and lack of obedience and respect toward parents, with some questionable sexual ethics thrown in for good measure, are making American companies a bundle from the Mexican market.

For example, there is a soft drink commercial played on Mexican television multiple times each day. A well-known American company produces this drink.

The commercial begins with a group of teenagers who are heading for an indoor swimming pool. On finding it closed, they quickly plan to break in—they plot to break the law. One of the young ladies whips out an instant camera, snaps a picture of the undisturbed pool, waits for it to develop, and then tapes the picture to the security camera. This, of course, is to fool the *adult* security guard--portrayed as a stupid dolt--into thinking all is well when he looks at his monitor.

That accomplished, the teens climb over the fence and head for the pool. Unknown to the partying teenagers, the wind blows the picture off the security camera, the security guard notices the intruders, and the jig is up. Instead of calling the police or running the teenagers off, the guard joins the party with the law-breaking adolescents.

Do you see what is wrong with the commercial? Do you see what it communicates to the Mexican people, especially Mexican teenagers?

"Having fun is something good. That which is good is desirable. The closed swimming pool is bad because it prevents me from getting that which is good for me.

83

Breaking into the swimming pool is a means to the end of having a fun time--something good. Therefore, the end justifies the means. The only bad or evil thing was that the pool was closed when I wanted to use it."

I am afraid this is the prevailing humanist philosophy--the end justifies the means. It affects all facets of today's American existence. "That which is right and good in the universe is that which benefits me. The only wrong or evil in the universe is that which denies me that which benefits me." Like it or not, this is what America has been spouting to its own unsuspecting public and then exporting to the world.

Another television commercial advertises an American company that makes a popular corn chip. The commercial begins in the morning with an unkempt young man of around 20 who looks as though he has been rolling in the hay with someone all night. This is exactly what he has been doing, as we find out later in the commercial. The young man acts slightly confused and disoriented--as though he is clueless how he came to be in this bed. He gets out of bed, pulls on only his pants, and leaves the bedroom clutching his bag of corn chips.

In the next scene, the young man shuffles into the dining room, where the man and lady of the house, with the grandmother, are sitting at the table eating breakfast. Also at the table is the *very* young daughter--obviously the young man's nighttime partner. The young man continues to munch on his corn chips. The girl's parents have shocked expressions on their faces at the sight of the shirtless, disheveled young man. He acknowledges no one save his roll-in-the-hay partner. He shuffles over to her and kisses her as though he plans to continue their nighttime activities right there in the dining room.

The commercial portrays the parents as too stupid and ineffectual to do anything other than sit with their mouths open in shock. The mother hides her eyes during the kiss while the grandmother looks on with a fiendishly amused grin on her face.

The kiss ends, the young man shuffles out the back door, and continues munching on his corn chips. The girl has a devilish smirk on her face and the grandmother stares at the young man's rear end with a lean and hungry look (this really freaks me out!).

I can easily recall when American TV would not show this crap. Now, it is commonplace. Americans no longer flinch at the sight of a bunch of kids breaking into a locked building. They no longer react with disgust when a commercial implies a young girl had a sexual encounter with her boyfriend under her parents' roof. People find these commercials cute, clever, and funny.

I would love for someone to tell me what the events in these commercials have to do with eating a certain brand of corn chip or drinking a certain brand of soft drink. What brilliant minds approved showing this rot? Does it increase sales of the products? If it does, then isn't this a salient testimony of how far American morality and ethics have declined? Now, America wants to export that low-level morality and ethics to the rest of the world by television advertising.

Another interesting development of the Americanization of Mexico is the arrival of large discount chains like Wal-Mart, Sam's Club, and Costco. Thanks to the North American Free Trade Agreement (NAFTA), these chains and others such as Office Depot, Home Depot, McDonalds, Burger King, Kentucky Fried Chicken, Domino's, Pizza Hut, and 7-Eleven operate inside Mexico's borders.

While the supporters make the argument that this results in lower-priced consumer goods, I am afraid they will have the same effect on small Mexican businesses that they did in small-town America.

Take Wal-Mart for example. This company is an American success story and makes as much as the Gross Domestic Product of some countries. Most of the money it earns is money the consumer formerly spent in the small mom-and-pop businesses that used to abound in America. Small businesses just cannot compete with a huge chain's volume buying power.

The result of huge chains moving into towns is that they kill most, if not all, of the existing businesses. Since most of the small businesses in small towns are in the downtown area, the advent of a huge discount chain makes the once-thriving downtown into a ghost town. These chains are destroying a way of life and reengineering society.

I can remember when life in America was like life still is in much of Mexico. I recall going with my mother to the small mom-and-pop neighborhood grocery stores, to the butcher, and to the bakery to do our shopping.

Some would suggest that this is a patronizing attitude. They would contend that wanting to keep small towns from achieving modern progress is to fulfill some patronizing need to keep the past alive. That's not it at all!

I cannot begin to fathom what would happen if a Wal-Mart Supercenter opened outside Guanajuato. The death of a centuries-old way of life would happen--overnight. Social reengineering would begin immediately. Mom-and-pop corner stores--the only means these people have had to make a living--would cease to exist.

Is it progress to kill off the only way of life a people have known for uncounted generations? What gives

American businesses the right to reengineer another country's culture?

If that is progress, according to the American social evolutionists, then I don't want any part of it.

Chapter Eight
Shocking Things

Why include a chapter on the shocking matters you might find if you expatriate to Mexico? A Canadian expatriate friend suggested this as an important topic to cover. His point was that a great many Americans and Canadians come to Mexico intending to live here more or less permanently. However, they have little idea of what to expect in day-to-day living.

That got me to thinking about culture shock and how so much of it stems from not knowing what to expect. My hope is that you will get a taste of some of the conditions that might shock you in Mexico.

Noise

On your first night in Mexico, you will undoubtedly make the discovery of just how noisy Mexico is. It is obvious the people here have a greater tolerance for a high volume of sound than people have in America.

The noise may be in the workman who plays his boom box loud enough so people for several blocks can enjoy the music too. Perhaps a maid, doing laundry in a rooftop laundry room, will play music (and sing along) loud enough to wake the dead. One cannot forget the roof dogs. They bark at just about everything that they see, and start their nightly chorus of barking and howling, which lasts for at least an hour.

Then, there are frequent parties and festivals to contribute to the noise level. Parties and festivals always include music, played at headache-inducing volumes. In addition, they are often with window-rattling, bone-jarring explosive charges. I'm not referring to the colorful fireworks you see on Independence Day. These are explosions that shake, rattle, and roll you out of a sound sleep at 6 a.m. and make you think that World War III has just begun outside your window.

It is odd, at least to me, that the Mexicans don't mind a noise level loud enough to jar the fillings out of the teeth of an average American. The louder the music, the more they enjoy it.

We thought we prepared ourselves for this fact of Mexican life before we moved here. Mexican friends in the U.S. told us about the noise level. We had experienced the noise factor during our fact-finding trip to Guanajuato to study Spanish. However, little did we know what was in store for us during our first several months here.

We secured a small but comfortable apartment in Guanajuato through an ad on the Internet. The landlord told us the apartment's location, but not knowing the various neighborhoods, we didn't have a clue what was waiting for us.

We moved in on August 1, 2003, a rainy but quiet day. The quietness amazed us, but we didn't know quiet was a rarity in that neighborhood.

The downtown area of Guanajuato is built along a ravine where the River Guanajuato flowed for centuries (engineers diverted from that area in 1901 after a devastating flood). Since the terrain is mountainous, much of Guanajuato looks like a bowl with the downtown area at the bottom of the bowl and houses built up the sides (an awesome feat of engineering skill). As a result, the bowl is like an amphitheater. Every sound is magnified and echoes around the bowl.

Our apartment was nearly at the top of one side of the bowl and was above the downtown area. As you can imagine, we could hear noise from everywhere in the bowl. As well as the traffic noise and the people noise, there are several churches in the bowl, all of which ring their bells every 15 minutes, to call people to mass, for weddings, for festivals, and for funerals.

Those churches, the barking dogs, and loud music coming from multiple directions would have been enough to cope with. However, we had another source of noise that was inescapable.

Less than two blocks away from our apartment was a small church called "The Church of Our Lady of Guadalupe." Not only do the church bells ring every 15 minutes, there are also multiple festivals held throughout the year, all requiring much enthusiastic bell ringing. We should have realized that this would be a popular church, despite its small size, because the Virgin of Guadalupe is Mexico's patron saint.

During December, there is a holiday called, "The Feast of the Virgin of Guadalupe." This holiday begins on December 1 and lasts until the Saint's day on December 12.

During this holiday period, every day begins with explosive charges and frequent bell ringing from about 5 a.m. until late evening. Every evening, many people congregate on the street leading to the church to carry the statue of the Virgin to the church. A band consisting of drummers and trumpet players accompanies the parade of people. The band plays, the people sing and chant prayers, the church bells ring nonstop, and the explosive charges rattle the windows until the statue of the Virgin reaches the church.

On December 12, the big party begins. Vendors set up booths along the whole street that leads to the church. People begin climbing the street early in the morning to take offerings of fruits, vegetables, and eggs to the Virgin. Various bands set up along the street, each trying to drown out the music of the others. The church bells ring continuously. It seems that most of Guanajuato's population congregates in the street throughout the day. It makes for a long and noisy (though fun) day.

No sleeping late during the first 2 weeks of December! In fact, the noise is so intensive during the daily parades and the party on December 12 that we could not hear each other when we tried to talk in our apartment. We could see each other's mouths move, but could not hear a single syllable.

We have since moved to a quieter part of town. There are still some barking dogs, and some traffic noise, but nothing compared with our first apartment. If noise is bothersome to you, then walk around several neighborhoods at various times of the day to find out how noisy each area is. Look for the presence of dogs and look for churches.

Beggars

In the Gospels, Jesus said the *poor* would always be with us. This is true on the streets of Mexico. Begging is a way a life for many people.

I don't know who these people are or where they are from originally. Many look like they belong to one of the indigenous (Indian) tribes. Most look in dire straits, while others look well fed and adequately clothed. We've heard that some beggars are part of a gypsy-type group who travel from town to town begging.

Guanajuato has a few pathetic-looking beggars. One fellow kneels on one knee with the other leg twisted at an unnatural angle behind him. He leans on a pair of crutches and holds his cap out for money. He looks so dirty and broken that people take pity on him and give him coins.

Early one morning, I was on my way to my Spanish class when I caught sight of this fellow. He was not in his usual kneeling position but was standing on his feet, crutches slung over his shoulder. He looked just fine. A miracle has happened and he has been healed, I thought. He was talking with a group of buddies and drinking something out of a bottle wrapped in a paper bag. Well, no miracle had occurred as I had thought. Later that day, I saw this fellow in his usual spot, kneeling on one knee, the other leg twisted unnaturally behind him, leaning on his crutches, and holding his cap out for pesos!

Some beggars are content to stake out a particular street corner or a particular doorway. Some move from place to place and some walk the streets. They hold their hands out, begging for coins to feed their children. Some are severely aggressive and will tug at your sleeve if you try to pass without giving them something. Some will beg in the restaurants where you are trying to have a meal, not just for money, but for food as well.

I feel that if you are on the street, you are fair game for beggars and vendors. However, if you pay good money to have a quiet and relaxing meal, you should not have to fend off beggars (or vendors, for that matter).

Here's something else to watch out for. We've seen beggars use small children as a sympathy card, "Won't you help me feed my baby?" Then, they take the money to the nearest kiosk and buy tobacco products! This is something we have seen, not just once, but many times.

I am convinced that when beggars or vendors see a gringo face, they assume the gringo has money to burn. Other expatriates have expressed the same opinion. At least two complete strangers have approached us and asked us to buy them tickets to other cities in Mexico. Other expatriates have had similar experiences.

Some beggars are not aggressive. They will sit or stand on the street, sing a song or play an instrument, and have a cup available for passersby to give a few coins. We will sometimes give a couple of pesos to these people because they are offering something in exchange, though the singing and playing are usually terrible.

The sad part is the begging children. They are almost always children of indigenous parents and are usually dirty, unkempt, and appear hungry. In addition, they are out begging and not attending school. They often sell chewing gum, candy, or flowers. These children can be extremely aggressive (no doubt taught by their parents' example), will follow you around, and continue to hound you. You will have to be firm and tell them, "No, gracias." If that doesn't work, then you will have to tell them, "Dejame en paz." which means, "Leave me in peace."

A great many tourists reinforce this begging behavior

by giving money to the beggars. I think it is a matter of personal choice whether you give money to the beggars.

Dogs

When we visited Guanajuato the first time, we noticed right away there were an incredible number of feral street dogs. They were starving, some had mange, and some were very aggressive. They would scatter trash everywhere looking for scraps of food to eat, they would beg people for handouts, and posed a health hazard.

When we moved here six months later, the state of affairs had not improved. Seemingly, many people in Guanajuato do not care for their dogs because they let them run loose in the streets and do not spay or neuter their dogs, which results in more unwanted dogs. In addition, many people do not vaccinate their dogs. If a family can no longer afford to feed the family pet, it is turned loose on the streets to fend for itself.

A couple of months later, we noticed a marked absence of feral dogs. It was just before the annual International Cervantino Festival, a time when there are a great number of tourists in town. We wondered if there was a connection, so we asked around. We found out that because the dogs are a menace and a health hazard, and the city does not want to lose the tourist trade during the festival as a result, the city decided to act. The rumor was that most of the feral dogs were rounded up, taken out in the countryside, and thrown off cliffs. I hope this was not true.

In 2004, the newspaper reported the city had to kill 3500 feral dogs by shooting them in the head. It is sad, but shooting them is much more humane than throwing them off cliffs where they may or may not survive.

Another issue that was strange to us was seeing many dogs kept on the roofs of houses. It made sense after we thought about it for a while. One reason is that few houses have yards in which to keep dogs. Another reason is the way people must build houses on the sides of the mountains. Many of the houses are connected side-by-side and stair-step up the mountainsides. The roof dogs provide security in case someone climbs from one house to the next to try to rob people. Unfortunately, many of these dogs are lonely because no one pays attention to them, some are not well fed, and some have no shelter to escape the sun and the rain.

Not everyone in Guanajuato treats his or her dogs badly. We have Mexican friends who do all the right things for their dogs. They spay or neuter them and keep them confined to the house. They vaccinate them, feed them premium dog food, and put them on a leash if they venture outside the house.

There is an effort in Guanajuato to raise money to offer free spay, neuter, and vaccination clinics for pet owners who cannot afford to pay. There are also people who rescue street dogs, pay for vaccinations, pay for dogs to be spayed, neutered or have other treatments and then find good homes for these rehabilitated animals. Many other Mexican cities have groups that make these types of humanitarian efforts.

Another dog-related problem has to do with their bathroom habits. In Guanajuato, there isn't enough grass for dogs to use as a bathroom. Therefore, the sidewalks and streets are the places where dogs leave their deposits.

This would not be so bad if dog owners would clean up after their pets. Most dog owners do not appear to notice the messes their dogs leave behind. In fact, people are appalled to see responsible dog owners cleaning up after their pets.

Remember to keep your eyes peeled and watch where you step while walking so you avoid these sidewalk hazards.

Heating and Air-Conditioning

The fact that we have no central heat or central air-conditioning in our house has shocked many of our American friends. They just cannot fathom how people can live without these modern comforts. In Guanajuato, the weather is so mild that we do not need either of these.

During the summer months, Guanajuato can be a bit humid since most of the yearly rainfall occurs then. We have found that using a box fan is enough to keep us cool. During January, the evenings and early mornings can be a bit chilly, so we use an oil-filled space heater.

As I wrote in the cost-of-living chapter, your electric bill will be low if you live in an area with a similarly mild climate. If you choose an area at a high elevation, you may need heat, but you will not need an air-conditioner. If you choose a beach or jungle area, you will probably need air-conditioning, but not a heater.

Shopping

Traditional Mexican shopping is almost a daily event. People visit the panaderia (bakery), the carniceria (butcher shop), the fruteria (fruit and vegetable shop), and the tienda de abarrotes (small grocery store). Most foods are fresh, not packaged, so they have a shorter shelf life. To us, Mexican foods taste better than their American counterparts.

Some of our American friends are appalled at the idea of shopping nearly every day and having to visit multiple stores instead of shopping weekly (or monthly) at just one supermarket. There are supermarkets in Mexico, but people prefer the friendly service in the smaller neighborhood shops and markets.

Product availability is another issue of the traditional Mexican shopping experience that would send most American shoppers into orbit. You cannot expect to find an abundance of American brands. If you do find some, they will cost more than Mexican brands. In addition, not all products, even Mexican brands, are available all the time. Therefore, if you see something you want or need, it is best to buy it right then. The next time you visit the store, the product may not be there and may never be in stock again.

If standing in long lines at a store sends your blood pressure through the roof, then think twice about expatriating to Mexico. Even if the line is short, you may have to wait for some time while the clerk and customers catch up on news and gossip. While Americans become angry and loud if they feel they are not given the service they want, Mexicans wait patiently and calmly until it is their turn.

Store hours in the small neighborhood shops and markets are another issue that can test your patience. I have to admit that I still struggle with this issue. Many stores do not post their hours of operation. Instead, they open when the owner arrives and close when the owner is ready to go home. The stores that do post their hours may or may not open and close on schedule. Sometimes a store will close for a day or two with no explanation or warning.

My wife needed some yarn to complete a project, but was unable to find what she needed. Finally, someone directed us to a shop that carried the yarn. We arrived, only to find the shop closed. There were no hours posted, so we decided to try again the next day at a different time of the day. The following day, we again found the shop closed.

This went on for several days though we arrived at various times of the morning, afternoon, and evening. One day, we walked by the shop on our way to somewhere else, when lo and behold, the shop was open! My wife bought her yarn and then asked the owner what her hours were. She shrugged her shoulders and replied,

"I open when I feel like it. If you need something in the future and the store is closed, just knock on the door and I will come down from my apartment upstairs and open for you."

Can you imagine how successful an American store would be with that method of operation? I love this country!

Obesity

It may shock you to see how few obese people there are in Guanajuato. It may be different in other regions of Mexico, but Guanajuato has a surprising number of fit-looking people.

On a recent trip to the U.S., we noticed again how fat Americans are. It was a huge contrast to what we were used to seeing in Guanajuato. We visited a shopping mall and noticed that a huge number of people were obese. In a Center for Disease Control and Prevention (CDC) 1999-2000 survey, it was estimated that 64% of U.S. adults were either overweight or obese. The CDC says that obesity in adults has increased by 60% over the past 20 years.

I would like to suggest several reasons for the disparity in weight between Mexicans and Americans.

One reason is car ownership. Americans regard cars as essentials of life whereas most Mexicans cannot afford to own cars. Mexicans walk; in America, walking is almost a forbidden action. Car ownership, in my view, has contributed to obesity in America. If you have ever watched American drivers in a mall or supermarket parking lot, you have seen people driving around endlessly looking for a close parking spot rather than parking further away and walking. Americans go to great lengths, wasting both time and gasoline, to avoid walking.

Another reason is the size of the portions and the size of the meals served at home and in restaurants. Instead of serving supersized portions as American restaurants do, Mexican restaurants serve small, but satisfactory portions. Also, the main meal, eaten around 2 p.m., consists of small portions of several foods. There will usually be a soup followed by a rice or pasta dish. The main course is a small piece of chicken or a small portion of an entrée, vegetables, and a salad. Tortillas or rolls usually accompany the meal. Dessert is normally fruit or pudding. Breakfast is something light such as juice or fruit, maybe an egg or yogurt, and coffee. Supper is equally light and may consist of a small portion of the main meal's entrée, a couple of enchiladas, tacos, or tamales.

A third reason for the disparity is that much of the food in Mexico is fresh, not refined, processed or packaged. There are very few frozen microwave dinners or packaged meals in Mexico. Those you can find are usually expensive. Americans are addicted to high-calorie, high-sodium, high-fat foods and rarely eat the recommended servings of fruits and vegetables.

Finally, Mexicans deal with stress far better than Americans do. One way Americans deal with stress is by eating--especially high-fat, high-sugar, high-calorie foods.

Mexicans have the attitude that work will get done when it gets done and whatever happens is in the hands of God, so why worry? As a result, most Mexicans eat to live and not to cope with stress.

Public Behavior

One issue that might be shocking is the delightful lack of public rage behavior in Mexico. In general, Mexicans know how to behave in public and do so with grace and humility.

I don't know what experiences you have had while growing up in the United States. Our experience has been seeing a culture of rage develop. People have forgotten how to treat one another with courtesy and patience.

After our February 2003 fact-finding trip came to end, we reluctantly boarded a plane in Leon, Guanajuato, to make our way back to Kansas City. In the Houston airport, we had to go through customs and change planes. After the grueling, 2-hour customs ordeal, we limped wearily through the airport to find the gate we needed for our connecting flight.

In the waiting area at our gate, we were trying to gain strength for the next leg of our journey. Suddenly, we were treated with an example of this rage behavior. Across the way at another gate, a shrieking madman was raging at the poor ticket agent. Apparently, he missed his flight and was not receiving the answers he wanted from the airline personnel. He cursed wildly, hands and arms flailing, face red, eyes bulging. We thought he was going to have a heart attack or a stroke! Finally, at the end of his rope, he threw his suitcases into the concourse (nearly taking out a few of his fellow travelers). He began kicking the wall and continued his cursing tirade. I turned to my wife and commented, "Welcome back to America!" She mournfully cried, "Do you think we can get back on the plane and return to Mexico?"

Now, correct me if I am wrong, but is this what America has become? Did we just leave what America refers to as a third world country to return to a developed country of raging madmen?

Another observation we made while trapped in the Houston airport was most of the people were angry, whining, and complaining. Now, I realize that airline travel is tiring and airports are uncomfortable, but do those facts require travelers to be unhappy? Everyone knows (or should know) there are long lines because of increased security and sometimes long waits for connecting flights, so why be unhappy and complain? Bring a book, read a paper, get something to eat and drink and relax!

Lest you dismiss these observations as isolated incidents in a stressful environment, try the following experiments. Go to your local mall, find a comfortable seat, and watch the masses. Listen to the complaining, the arguing, the rebellion against parents, and the rage behavior. Or, get into your car and cruise on the highways and streets. Watch how people act when they have to wait for a stoplight, wait for another person to park or turn, when someone cuts them off, or when someone won't let them change lanes.

Is this any way to live?

I am happy to report that we have not seen one Mexican display this behavior. No raging, no drive-by shootings, no screaming matches, and no cursing fits--nothing. If it happens, it happens in private. The only "rage" behavior we have witnessed in Mexico is people honking their car horns when stuck in traffic.

Modes of Transportation

Most people here walk when they need to go somewhere. The number of people on the streets as well as their legs and buns of steel prove this fact. The mountainous terrain here in the heartland builds strong bodies and powerful cardiovascular systems. We have seen many elderly people hauling huge, backbreaking bags and bundles up the steeply sloped streets without breaking a sweat. We are much younger than some of these people, yet we can barely make it up the same streets (with frequent rest stops and without a single bag) without feeling that we need a tank of oxygen at the summit!

So, what do you do when the weather is inclement? What if you have groceries to carry or you want to go somewhere that is too far to walk? If you don't own a car, you have two choices: buses or taxis.

Riding the buses can be a shocking experience for several reasons. First, you have to be sure the bus you choose actually goes to your desired destination. You need to ask the bus driver if your destination is on his route even if the sign on the bus says that it is. We have taken buses that listed our destination on the route on the front of the bus, only to find ourselves in Timbuktu with a driver who is not planning on going back into the city until his next shift!

Second, many of the bus drivers drive like madmen. You have to remember that Guanajuato's streets are narrow and were originally planned for horse and burro traffic. In addition, people park their cars along the streets (sometimes two and three deep!), leaving precious little space for the buses to pass. Many of the drivers think their bus is the only vehicle on a four-lane-wide highway and drive like Indy 500 racecar drivers!

Finally, when the bus arrives at a bus stop, you cannot dally for even a second. If you hesitate, the bus may leave without you. Worse yet, you may have one foot on the bus step and the other on the ground when the driver takes off. Always grab the rail beside the bus' door when you prepare to board. That way, if the driver decides to rush off to his next destination, you will be able to hang on for dear life and eventually pull yourself up into the bus. You laugh, but we have seen this (and experienced it) too many times to count.

Taxis are more expensive than taking the bus (25 pesos versus 2 ½ pesos). However, you can be assured of having a seat in a taxi. More often than not, you will have to stand in the bus (hanging on to the grab bar for dear life as the driver whips around corners at lightning speed!). However, taxi drivers learned their driving skills from the same source as the bus drivers. Many drive too fast, take curves too quickly, and pass everything on the road (even on blind hills).

Now, here is where pedestrians and public transportation intersect. If you choose walking as your manner of transportation, you must keep the driving habits of the bus and taxi drivers in the forefront of your mind. Why, you ask? Because they drive too fast and too recklessly on the streets, they do not always watch where they are going, and they are not always careful when turning corners.

Guanajuato has several spots that are dangerous for pedestrians. The most dangerous places are in the downtown area on a street named Cantarranas. This street is dangerously narrow with very narrow sidewalks. In addition, it has several sharp corners. When you hear or see a bus coming while you are walking around these sharp corners, either run for your life or jump into a doorway or store. Otherwise, you will be squashed because the buses do not have enough room to turn without sending their back ends fishtailing over the sidewalk.

A last warning for pedestrians is in order here. Not only do you have to watch for piles of doggie-do left in your path, you also have to watch for holes and uneven paving. Many of the sidewalks are cobblestone and thus uneven. We have seen both Mexicans and gringos fall victim to the dangers of navigating the sidewalks.

(Thankfully, the city is replacing some of the cobblestone streets and sidewalks with brick and flat paving stones, so walking should be a little less dangerous in the future.)

Time

I just want to mention this theme briefly since I have covered it elsewhere in the book.

Mexicans have a different worldview or philosophy of time than you may find in other parts of the world. Time is less important to Mexicans than it is to Americans. In fact, Mexicans find it sad that Americans are chained to the clock.

Most Mexicans never show up on time (on gringo time anyway) for anything. They don't open their stores at the posted time (though they open eventually), they don't arrive for appointments on time, and they don't come to class on time.

We took several months of Spanish classes at one of the local language schools when we first moved to Guanajuato. As time-controlled gringos, we always arrived at the school early for class--sometimes 15 or 20 minutes early. This was true of most of the other students as well. As the hour approached for the classes to begin, we gringos would be milling around and checking our watches. However, the teachers had yet to arrive. Finally, the teachers would trickle in 5 to 10 minutes late with nary an apology. After a few weeks, we relaxed and stopped fretting about the failure of the teachers to arrive on time.

If you make an appointment for a contractor or workman to come to your house to do repairs, don't expect him to be on time. Be patient--he will arrive eventually. A friend hired a painter to paint his house. The painter came every day around 1 p.m. and worked until 6 or 7. One day, when he was nearly finished with the job, he told our friend that he would be back the next day at 1 p.m. to finish the job. The next day, 1 p.m. came and went. Our friend was still waiting at 6, but the painter never arrived. Finally, three days later, the painter showed up at 1 p.m. as though the intervening days had not passed! No apologies, no explanations, no hint that anything was amiss.

One odd thing about time is that people are rarely on time for anything, yet they are the fastest walkers we have ever seen! Pedestrians here walk at a near-run and will bowl you over if you get in their way--always accompanied by a polite, "Con permiso." ("Excuse me."). We often wonder just where they are going in such a hurry. It is not because they want to be on time for a class or an appointment.

A last note: if you are invited to someone's house or to a restaurant at a certain time, ask your hosts if they mean the hour "en punto" (on the dot) or if they mean up to 30 minutes after the specified hour. You can also ask if they mean "gringo time" (the hour on the dot) or "Mexican time".

Street Vendors

Most street vendors have stationary kiosks from which they sell various goods such as newspapers, magazines, candy, tobacco products, fruit, tacos, sandwiches, toys, and fruit drinks. You approach these stands if they interest you.

Other vendors do not have stands, but roam around the streets and parks selling jewelry, rugs, serapes (colorful woven blankets), flowers, candy, gum, and junky trinkets. Most are pleasant people and are not aggressive. Some, however, are aggressive and will not take no for an answer.

One of our first experiences with these roving vendors occurred while we were sitting in the city's main plaza. A man approached us and tried to sell us a serape. He was a small man, but he waved his serapes and rugs in front of us with all the skill and finesse of a matador. As we did not speak or understand much Spanish at the time, we were neither able to understand him nor make ourselves understood. We did not want to buy a serape, but had not yet learned that a simple, "No, gracias." is enough to send a vendor on his way.

He must have tried every sales pitch in his repertoire to get us to buy his serape. We tried, in our broken Spanish, to explain that we did not want to buy one, we did not need one, nor did we have room to carry one home in our suitcase. Our endeavors only spurred him on to more elaborate pitches. This went on for 25 minutes. I am sure he thought he would wear us down eventually! The more we said, "No.", the more he persisted. Just when we thought we had finally convinced him that we weren't interested, he whipped out a lighter and started to set the blanket on fire!

Horrified that we had upset this man so much that we drove him to burn his blanket up in despair, we made a quick exit! We later learned that they make these serapes of 100% wool--wool does not burn. This gentleman was trying to show that his products were not made of inferior acrylic, but were indeed wool!

A word to the wise: if you do not want to buy a vendor's goods, just say, "No, gracias." and leave it at that.

Scorpions

It just may surprise and shock you that Mexico has one of the most dangerous scorpions in the *world*. The most dangerous ones are in the deserts of the Middle East and Africa. This is worth mentioning because, if you choose to live in a desert area of Mexico, you will find scorpions.

Now, don't panic and decide you could never live in a country that has dangerous scorpions. If you live in the United States, you should know it has a dangerous scorpion, called the Bark scorpion, which lives in the desert Southwest.

Over our first six months in Guanajuato, we found four large scorpions crawling across the floor of our apartment. Quickly, we became interested in how to get rid of them.

Mexico has some harmless scorpions as well as the more dangerous variety. Learning to distinguish one from the other can be an exercise in futility. The locals will tell you the "brown" scorpions are harmless but the "tan" ones are dangerous. I don't know about you, but "brown" and "tan" are too similar for me to distinguish at a moment's notice from several feet away! Our advice is, if you see a scorpion, don't stand there trying to decide if it is dangerous or not--just kill it!

Keep your house free of the insects that scorpions prey on. Keep your house and yard clutter-free. Always check your bedding before hopping under the covers and shake out your shoes and clothes before putting them on. Look before sticking your hand somewhere. If you follow these tips, you will likely avoid a sting.

If a scorpion stings you, try to get a look at the size and color of the scorpion. Put ice on the sting and get to the nearest clinic or emergency room for treatment. Mexican doctors are knowledgeable about scorpions and their stings and will know how to treat you.

One word of caution: if you are in the market for inexpensive leather goods, Leon, Guanajuato, is a good place to look for bargains. However, much of the leather comes from the state of Durango, where there is a large amount of the dangerous variety of scorpions. Don't let this deter you from buying leather items. Just check all seams and pockets carefully before wearing the item. Also, check under and around shoe insoles before wearing them.

Chapter Nine
Guanajuato

In Chapter One, I wrote the primary reason for moving to Mexico was because of my chronic health problems.

Cost of living and safety were also issues. But why did we choose Guanajuato? Why did we choose the heartland rather than another location with more gringo expatriates? Perhaps some background will help.

The state of Guanajuato, located in the geographical center of Mexico, is surrounded by the states of San Luis Potosi, Queretaro, Jalisco, and Michoacan. Forty-five minutes west of Guanajuato's capital, also named Guanajuato, is the Guanajuato International Airport (BJX). Other cities in the state include San Miguel de Allende, Dolores Hidalgo, and Leon.

The name, Guanajuato, originally spelled "Guanaxuato" or "Quanaxjuato", is the Tarascan Indian word for "Hill of Frogs". No one knows exactly why the tribe gave the area this name. One story is that, on looking at the terrain, they decided nothing could live here except frogs. Another story is that some of the rocks on the mountain peaks around the area looked like frogs.

Founded in 1548 close to the Rio Guanajuato, the city is nestled in a valley surrounded by mountains. Standing in the downtown area is like being in the bottom of a bowl. Breathtakingly beautiful Baroque and Neoclassical buildings, many of which were homes during the Spanish occupation, fill the bottom of the bowl. The discovery of rich silver mines in the area provided the wealth to produce the grandeur that is still evident today. Some consider the architecture of Guanajuato to be the most beautiful in Central and South America.

Looking up from the downtown area, you witness a remarkable feat of engineering skill. In Guanajuato, the residential areas surrounding the heart of the city had nowhere to go but up the sides of the mountains. It seems the builders used every available inch of the mountainsides. Houses stair-step up the sides and follow the terrain in undulating rows. In some places, the roof of one house is at the next house's foundation.

Many of these houses are not accessible by car. The only way to gain access to them is by narrow, twisting callejones. These are cobblestone alleyways, some containing steps carved into the rocky mountainside, which snake up to the summits.

The city of Guanajuato has been called the crown jewel of Mexico's heartland. In 1988, UNESCO declared Guanajuato "Patrimonio Cultural de la Humanidad" (Cultural Legacy of Mankind). Since it is a World Heritage Site, any new construction or remodeling in the historic center must conform to strict rules. Also, they must build gas stations and other modern buildings outside the city center. For these reasons, the city keeps its historic charm.

The silver mines discovered here put Guanajuato on the map. At one point, silver made Guanajuato the commercial and financial center of central Mexico. The silver mines once supplied the world with one-third of its silver wealth, much of it going into the coffers of the Spanish royalty. Most of the mines stopped producing in the 1800s, but a few continue to be active today.

Guanajuato played a unique role in Mexico's struggle for independence from Spain. The mines made many of the Spanish overlords wealthy at the expense of the Mexican workers. Finally, the people rebelled.

In 1810, Catholic priest, Miguel Hidalgo y Costilla, organized and led a ragtag army that consisted of farmers and peasants. They began their quest for independence in the city called Dolores (later renamed Dolores Hidalgo) with Hidalgo's impassioned speech, "El Grito", on the steps of the parish church on the night of September 10, 1810. The army marched from place to place, slaughtering most of the Spanish as they went.

Hidalgo, known as the "Father of Mexican Independence", led his troops (which numbered around 20,000 by then) into Guanajuato, where the Spanish were barricaded in the gigantic granary, called the "Alhondiga de Granaditas". The Spanish were able to hold out against the rebel army until September 28, when a brave young miner stormed the wooden doors, setting them ablaze. This allowed the insurgents access to the granary where they killed everyone inside.

The city erected a monument to honor the brave miner named, Juan Jose de los Reyes Martinez Amaro, nicknamed "El Pipila". The statue overlooks the center of town. It provides a magnificent view of the city, one that is popular with photographers. If you are healthy, you can climb to the monument by way of the Callejon de Calvario, just east of Teatro Juarez on Calle Sopeña. For those who are not inclined to make the half-hour climb, there is a funicular (cable car), located behind Teatro Juarez, which will take you up for a few pesos.

Trying to find your way around the city of Guanajuato can be confusing and frustrating. Instead of building the streets in a grid pattern as many cities do, the city planners had to build the streets to fit the topography of the land. The streets wind around in various directions and sometimes end abruptly. To make it even more confusing, many streets change names every so often. In addition, signs do not mark many streets. The tourist office can give you an assortment of maps that are helpful, though some are not drawn to scale and some have few, if any, street names.

A unique feature that you will find in Guanajuato is the series of subterranean tunnels. Some of the tunnels follow the old riverbed. After a devastating flood in 1901, city engineers diverted the river away from the city to prevent further flooding. In the 1960s, engineers converted the original riverbed to an underground street. Since then, the city has built more tunnels to try to alleviate the traffic-clogged aboveground streets.

If you ride or walk through the tunnels in the downtown area, you will see brick arches close to the ground. These are visible traces of the buildings that existed in centuries past, but were damaged by flooding. Eventually, people built other buildings on top of them. There are legends that many of the people who lived and worked in these buildings have not been able to find their eternal rest. Instead, they roam the underground streets, tunnels, and buildings.

For an interesting look at a piece of this "city under a city", visit the recently uncovered Claustro de San Pedro de Alcantara (Convent of St. Peter of Alcantara) across from the Jardin de la Union. Currently, workers have only uncovered the convent's courtyard and a small area of the church's sacristy. There are plans to try to restore as much of the convent and church as possible. However, this may prove difficult since the San Diego Church and Teatro Juarez were built on top of these buildings.

Though the city is a bit confusing to navigate, it is a good place to amble wherever the sidewalk or alley takes you. You never know what interesting sight you will find around the next bend. If you find yourself high above the city without a clue where you are, don't panic. Just go down the mountain until you reach the downtown area at the bottom.

Instead of having one main plaza, Guanajuato has numerous parks scattered throughout the city. Some have gazebos where bands play regularly. Some are little more than a couple of benches. Most are surrounded by shops, restaurants, and sidewalk cafes. They are inviting places to sit, have a drink or snack, and watch the world go by.

Because of frequent flooding and rebuilding over the centuries, Guanajuato has more of a European look and feel than the other colonial cities in Mexico. Also, because many of the Spanish who came to exploit the wealth of the silver mines came from the Andalusia region of Spain, the city has some Moorish influences. An Italian friend of ours, when viewing pictures of Guanajuato, commented that it looked like many of the hillside towns in Italy.

Guanajuato's weather is second-to-none. Phrases such as "unbelievably nice" and "indescribably lovely" come to mind. It is conducive to good physical as well as mental health. All the guidebooks say that Guanajuato has "eternal springtime".

On our first Christmas Day in Mexico, we ate breakfast on our terrace while gazing at the neighbor's orange tree (bursting with ripe oranges) and then took a stroll around town wearing shorts and short-sleeved shirts. It was very different from what we had experienced on Christmas Days in Kansas City!

Most days are sunny and warm, but not too warm. The high temperatures rarely are above the mid-80s and the low temperatures are rarely below the upper-40s. Even during the winter, the daytime will be warm enough to wear short-sleeved shirts, though with jeans instead of shorts. The nighttime temperatures are cool, but you will not need more than a lined windbreaker or heavy sweater if you venture outside.

There is a rainy season that begins in late May and lasts until mid-September. Even during this time, it rarely rains all day and usually does not rain every day. However, some of these downpours can be heavy and can result in mudslides.

Around 40% of the northern and eastern parts of the state of Guanajuato have a *steppe* climate, which means that evaporation exceeds precipitation. As a result, mostly desert shrub, thistle, and cactus grow here. The rest of the state has a *temperate* climate. This is a medium climate where oak forests, pine trees, and grazing land predominate.

In both climates, frost and hailstorms occur, but only for a few days each year. Frost usually occurs in the highest elevations and rarely on the streets and sidewalks of the city. Snow is rarely seen in this area and then only in the high elevations.

A feature that attracted us to Guanajuato is that it is a *genuine* Mexican town. By that, I mean it does not have

American fast-food establishments (except for Domino's Pizza) and it keeps its traditional Mexican character and values. It has largely escaped the infiltration of America's devolved sense of democracy, human rights, sexual ethics, and commercialism. Sadly, there are towns, formerly with genuine Mexican characters, that have changed because of the influences of the expatriates who settled in them.

One day, we met a gringo couple who were planning to expatriate to Mexico. They were looking for a traditional Mexican town where they could experience the culture and practice the language. On recommendations from friends, they visited some of the areas where expatriates congregate. Their comment was that it would be "too easy" to live in these areas because so many people speak English. They did not think they would be able to become fluent in Spanish if they chose one of these areas. Also, they commented the people (Mexican and expatriates alike) seemed unhappy in these areas.

Another feature that attracted us to Guanajuato is that it is wonderfully slow-paced and time appears to stand still here. People are not in a hurry and take time to chat with friends and neighbors on the street. The centuries-old buildings march alongside the cobblestone streets. Some people still use horses and burros for transportation and as pack animals, much as the inhabitants did in centuries past. It is not unusual to see a father taking his son to school on horseback or by burro. Burros carrying firewood and bags of soil are common sights in the streets, even in the downtown area.

Though Guanajuato has a slow pace compared with many Mexican cities, the introduction of motor vehicles has taken away some of its former tranquility. Many people own cars, but car ownership is not as prevalent here as in the United States. People always fill the sidewalks, unlike in the United States, where it is rare to see people walking. Also, people use public transportation instead of driving cars.

If you decide to bring a car to Mexico, you will need Mexican car insurance. Your American car insurance will not cover you in Mexico. You will not need a Mexican driver's license unless your U.S. license expires and you don't renew it. If you drive your car to Mexico and enter with a tourist visa, you will have to exit Mexico with the same car within the time period marked on the visa. Don't forget to keep all the paperwork you received when you entered Mexico. The customs officials will need to keep some of it when you exit Mexico. If you don't have it, the customs official may fine you.

You will also have to find a place to park your car if your house or apartment does not have a garage, carport, or a designated parking spot. While you may be able to find a free parking space close to your house or apartment, you may not be able to find one every time you return from an outing. In addition, you have to find a place to park at your destination—usually not an easy task. Parking garages exist, but they are expensive and are usually not convenient to your house or apartment. A friend pays $50 a month to park his car in a lot. It is so far from his house that he has to use public transportation to get back home from the lot.

One reason we chose Guanajuato was that it is small enough to be able to walk from our house to just about anywhere in town. In addition, walking is excellent exercise. People who exercise regularly live longer than people who are sedentary. Living in Guanajuato without a car forces you to walk, which benefits your health.

The people of Guanajuato are another draw. The people are used to the presence of foreign students and tourists, so are accepting of foreigners. Since the population of expatriates is so small, the locals have not been "burned" by foreigners as has happened in some of the regions where expatriates congregate.

We feel the community has accepted us as though we have been living here all our lives. After our first six months of living in Guanajuato, we had to go back to the border to renew our tourist visas. We never thought to tell the neighbors that we were going to visit a friend in Texas and we would return in 2 weeks. We arrived home, unpacked, and then headed out to the store for groceries. Neighbors and shopkeepers rushed out to the street to hug and kiss us! They had all been worried about us since they had not seen us for 2 weeks. They didn't know what had happened to us and thought that we had returned to the States permanently.

Does that happen in your neighborhood and in the stores where you shop when you are absent for some time? We still wonder if our neighbors in our apartment building in Kansas City even notice that we no longer live there!

Because Guanajuato is a university town, there are hosts of cultural activities throughout the year. Fine art films, art exhibitions, dance performances, plays, and performances by the University Symphonic Orchestra are just some of the activities you can enjoy. Each February, the restaurant association of Guanajuato hosts a Paella Festival, complete with Spanish music, flamenco dancers, and at least 10 kinds of paella. In March 2005, Guanajuato hosted Latin America's first Medieval Festival. It was a success and officials plan to make it an annual event.

The largest cultural event is the International Cervantino Festival, held for 3 weeks each October. This is a festival that celebrates the arts. Each year, the festival features one of Mexico's 31 states as well as 1 or 2 foreign countries. Artists, musicians, artisans, and dancers come to Guanajuato to display their skills.

The festival began in the 1950s with university students performing short dramas in Spanish in honor of Miguel de Cervantes y Saavedra, author of Don Quixote. The students performed these dramas in a plaza called, "Plaza de San Roque". The plaza, complete with bleachers and lighting, is still the site of many performances during the festival.

In 1972, the festival became an annual event. Since then, the number of participants and spectators has grown with each passing year. In 2004, the city reported that around 2500 artists performed for over 47,000 spectators in over 100 events.

During the festival, the event locations are filled to overflowing. Some events are free, so you need to stake out a seat a couple of hours or so in advance. For other events, you need to buy tickets that cost between 15 and 350 pesos each. Tickets sell out months in advance, so you will probably want to check with Ticketmaster (Mexico) beginning in July. A note of advice here: not only do the tickets sell out early, the hotels also are booked well in advance.

The festival has fallen out of favor with many of the locals in recent years. They call it a celebration of the art of drunkenness instead of a celebration of the arts. Unfortunately, though most of the spectators come to Guanajuato to experience the music, dance, plays, and arts; many come to engage in a three-week drinking session (among other activities.) These people do not share the conservative public behavior ethic the locals uphold. They engage in public drunkenness, rude behavior, fighting, doing, and selling drugs as well as other activities that are against the law. The police make many arrests during this festival, but it seems the same groups of nefarious individuals show up year after year. Some locals leave town during the festival to avoid the craziness that accompanies it.

During our first Cervantino festival, we discovered that hippies are alive and well. They poured into Guanajuato in their freaky, filthy clothes, their wild hair, and their questionable ethical behavior. They slept in the parks and on the streets, used the streets and sidewalks as bathrooms, smelled as if they had never used a bar of soap, and were outrageously loud. The police made many arrests for improper public behavior.

Post-Cervantino, the city falls back into its traditional routines. I can just see the merchants counting their Cervantino loot and the locals mopping their brows and breathing a sigh of relief that the wild party is over for another year.

Finally, there are several charming things about Guanajuato that confirmed our decision to choose it as our new home. One is the presence of the small, family-owned corner markets. These remind us of how people shopped when we were growing up. It is far more personal to go to your neighborhood stores where you know the owners than shopping at an impersonal supermarket where you rarely know anyone's name. Some contend that supermarkets in a town are a sign of progress. It is progress, but at what expense?

Another charming event is going to the movies. Guanajuato has two multi-screen movie theaters as well as a theater that sometimes shows fine art films.

A ticket costs 30 pesos (about $2.70 USD) every day except Wednesday when the cost is 18 pesos (about $1.60 USD). The concessions are just as inexpensive. A can of pop is less than a dollar and a bag of popcorn is less than

$1.50. A Mexican-brand candy bar is less than 50 cents.

Unlike the staff in many movie theaters in the United States, the workers here seem glad that you came to their theater. The ticket sellers and takers are always friendly and smiling. The concession-stand employees snap to attention when you approach the counter and treat you as though you are important.

Though these theaters are modern, multi-screen cinemas, they still remind us of going to the movies when we were growing up. Sometimes the sound track is a bit scratchy (which makes the Spanish a bit more difficult than usual to understand) just like the movies sounded in our youth. Also, just when the horrible monster is about to eat the hero, the movie stops and the lights come on. The first time we witnessed this, we thought the movie projector was broken. The rest of the audience ran out of the theater while we sat in shock. Were we going to have to come back another day to see the entire movie? As we were discussing this, the audience returned to the theater, the lights went out and the movie continued. The projectionist just had to change the reels! I don't remember that occurring at the movies since I was a child.

Finally, something that is charming but did not affect our decision to move here is that Guanajuato has a lighthouse! Now, if you have looked at a map of Mexico and located Guanajuato, you will know the city is landlocked and surrounded by mountains. There isn't an ocean within 300 miles! Why did someone think that Guanajuato needed a lighthouse? Did someone plan to build a canal across Mexico from the Pacific Ocean to the Gulf of Mexico at some point and think that Guanajuato would have ship traffic?

Someone told us the lighthouse was a gift to Guanajuato from the Mexican Navy. In the 1930s, each department of the federal government gave Guanajuato a gift. The Navy couldn't give Guanajuato a ship (there are only a couple of shallow reservoirs here—nothing big enough to hold a ship), so they decided the only item they could give was the lighthouse. The light still works and is turned on from time to time. It is a strange sight!

So, there you have it. Those are the reasons we chose Guanajuato over any other city in Mexico.

Chapter Ten
Learn Spanish

Americans will all but have a nervous breakdown at the thought of having to learn a foreign language. There are studies you can read online about the emotional problems college students suffer from trying to fulfill the foreign language requirement for their degree program.

When I was at the University of Kansas, back in the prehistoric times, the school of Liberal Arts had 3 degree programs from which to choose. We could choose the Bachelor of Arts, the Bachelor of Science, or the Bachelor of General Studies. The Bachelor of General Studies was popular because there was no foreign language requirement. Every single person I knew in the Bachelor of General Studies program was there to avoid taking a foreign language.

Why are Americans so afraid to learn a foreign language? Why do they go to such extraordinary lengths to avoid it? Some of those I knew in college would switch to the Bachelor of General Studies degree late in their degree programs after failing to fulfill the language requirement, thus delaying graduation.

The first reason, I think, an American would rather run and hide in a cave than become bilingual is the result of the dumbing down in American public schools. Imagine trying to learn the parts of speech in Spanish if you haven't a clue what they are in English. If you don't know a direct object from an indirect object, then your terror would be most understandable.

The second reason that Americans freak out at learning a new language is because of the methods used. The way teachers teach language can make all the difference.

I took Spanish in high school (1970) and college (1975). I recall the boring and mind-numbing approach the teachers used (and still use today). They issue you a huge textbook, a workbook that is about as interesting as watching paint dry, and some audiotapes with a native speaker reciting the mindless textbook dialog. Now, doesn't that make you want to run out to the Junior College and enroll in a foreign language course?

Furthermore, the gist of the course will be to memorize endless lists of vocabulary words, rules of grammar, and that mindless dialog. You will forget almost everything after the course and you will *not* be able to speak the language.

To make this a tantalizingly exciting learning event in your life, you will most likely have a *non-native* speaker instructor who will drone on and on in an American accent making the learning operation even more difficult. To learn grammar *first* is to put the cart before the horse.

What learning grammar first, as the primary step in language attainment, will do for you is enable you to become a linguist of the language. You will be able to *exegete* a piece of written text, but not speak the language. If that is your goal, then fine. However, if you want to speak the language, then you need the same approach you used, unknowingly, when you were a child learning your native language. You need spoken fluency *before* learning grammar! This, I realize, flies in the face of traditional foreign language education in America. But, you need to get this: The "horse" is the spoken fluency of language learning, and the "cart" is the learning grammar. Confused? Good, keep reading!

Have you ever considered how well most normal children speak English long before they reach the first grade? Or, even long before they can read a word of their native language? Just think how much information a 6-year-old child can communicate when they enroll in first grade.

Once, while trying to demonstrate this to a friend, I flagged down his busy little 7-year-old and asked her to walk *through* the kitchen door, which she did. Then I asked her to come back *into* the living room, which she did. I then asked her to explain what she had just done. She was 100% accurate in explaining that she had just followed my directions of walking *through* the door and then back *into* the living room. I then asked her to tell us what a preposition was—-she, of course, did not know.

Though she couldn't define the part of speech, preposition, how do you suppose she knew what *through* and *into* meant? How do you think she obviously mastered what those two parts of speech meant to follow my directions? And, not only that, how was she able to use them to describe her actions to us? Do you think she enrolled in a grammar course with a textbook, workbook, tapes?

She learned them, and everything else she knows about English as a 7-year-old, from listening to tens of thousands-- if not more--of repetitions of the target language in her little world. Long before she would know the names of the parts of speech, she knew how to use them. Perhaps with occasional errors, but with consistent fluency. When she finally starts formal grammar instruction, it will codify or define what she already knows. The formal instruction will fine-tune and correct errors. But, the point is that she had a high degree of spoken fluency long before she began a formal study of the grammar!

If you are studying a foreign language to gain spoken fluency, beginning with a grammar course is not going to help you reach your goal. This is as unnatural as it would be to enroll your toddler in an English grammar course so he or she can learn how to speak English. I mean, think about this! It would be putting the cart (grammar) before the horse (spoken fluency). A child begins the formal study of grammar of their native language already equipped with a high degree of spoken fluency. It is so important to get this concept.

As a potential expatriate to Mexico, I cannot overemphasize learning Spanish as your first priority! This will do more to reduce culture shock than anything else I can think of. In fact, I am convinced that learning Spanish will do more to raise your standing in the eyes of the locals than anything else will. What you are communicating to them is that their language is important enough to you for you to put the blood, sweat, and tears into mastering it!

If you want to expatriate to Mexico and have these wonderful, dear people accept you; *do whatever it takes* to learn Spanish!

You may want to offer the objection that an adult who wants to learn a language can already read a textbook and follow directions. I grant you that point. But, all that method will get the adult learner is an ability to read a piece of written text in the target language. It will make you a translator of written text. That's all!

A few years ago, I got it into my head that I wanted to learn *Koine* Greek. This is the ancient Greek dialect of which the New Testament is written in. I took my coursework from a seminary in Fort Worth, Texas. The material I received was a textbook, a workbook, and tapes. Because I could read and follow directions, I did well in memorizing long lists of vocabulary words and grammar rules. I eventually developed the skill to read portions of the New Testament in its original language. Just like learning Latin, I engaged in an exercise that taught me to wrestle with the *written* text. It did not equip me to speak one word of anything (besides, Koine Greek is no longer a spoken language).

Someone once told me the area of the brain involved in absorbing spoken language is different from the area that learns and absorbs facts like grammar rules and Word definitions. This makes some sense to me!

For the sake of argument, let's say that this is correct. Let's agree the area of the brain that learns spoken fluency is not the same area that memorizes long lists of vocabulary words and grammar rules. If this is true, then what are we doing beginning our learning of a second language with a textbook, a workbook, and tapes? Doesn't it make sense to begin with the same process in learning a second language that you did in learning your native language? Isn't this a no-brainer?

Note, I am making the point of not putting the *cart* before the *horse*. The horse is the natural, fluid procedure by which we develop spoken fluency. The cart is grammar. I hope that you understand that I am not pooh-poohing grammar. I'm not. It is that grammar has its place—behind the horse! The horse (spoken fluency) comes first, and pulls the cart (grammar). Are you getting this?

"Children who acquire a second language at a young age usually have considerable experience in listening to utterances in the foreign language. In addition to having considerably more listening experience than adults, children, as they are learning a second language, are not placed into a position in which they must talk. As they are acquiring the second language they do little talking. They mostly listen. This period of time, usually six months to one year, is called the silent period. During the silent period, children listen carefully to the meaning of the sentences and to how words are pronounced. When they begin to talk, they have largely mastered the basic fundamentals of the language."[6]

Even as adult learners of a second language, we need our own "silent period". This is the natural process of language learning whether you are a child or adult. To try to bypass it will result in failure.

Long before adults are in a position of having to speak in the target language, they need, as do children, this "silent period" of intensive listening.

Some would argue that this is what conversation classes are for. The problem with conversational classes is that they are full of students, just like you, who can't pronounce the sounds of the language, make frequent mistakes, and don't

---

[6] (International Linguistics Corporation; www.learnables.com/learnables.html)

know the necessary vocabulary. Conversational practice works best with a private native-speaker tutor. But, how many of us can afford that? In a traditional conversational class, you spend most of your time listening to your nonfluent classmates mispronouncing the language. This will, in the end, short-circuit the learning process.

"...conversational practice is only useful after an excellent understanding of the foreign language has been acquired." (Ibid).

Doesn't it make sense, if there were a method available that mirrored, as closely as possible, natural language learning, to use it? Does this sound like a sales pitch? Well, it is! But, I have absolutely no financial interest in this whatever. Nor does any member of my family. In fact, you could search high and low, but you will never find any financial connection between me and what I am about to tell you. The methods I am about to recommend to you worked for me. They work—that is my motive. They will work for anyone who isn't brain-dead.

There is a way to learn Spanish painlessly, fluidly, and naturally. There are two programs available on the market which do exactly what I've been explaining in this chapter, which I've used, and I highly recommend. Both of these programs teach you the target language in the precise manner you learned your native language.

The first program, published by the International Linguistics Corporation, is called *Learnables*. This system uses the same methods you unconsciously used when you learned your native language—watching and listening. In all five levels of their Spanish course, you listen to a series of tapes, all spoken by a native speaker, describing the action in a cartoon drawing. For example, "El niño esta comiendo." You will hear this sentence spoken, by a native speaker in the target language, while looking at a drawing of a boy eating. You may not initially understand the meaning of any of these words, but at the end of the lesson, you will.

This method is so brilliantly crafted that it can teach you some of the different tenses. This course is designed to mimic the "silent period" where all you do is listen. You learn an enormous amount of vocabulary as well as grammar (naturally!) with action-filled cartoon drawings of real-life events. You do no talking. You just listen--the "silent period". Just how you learned your native language.

I was once in a conversation where I couldn't recall how to say something in Spanish. I could remember the cartoon drawing action depicting what it is I wanted to say. Suddenly, the phrase popped into my head. This method works!

Once you've completed all five levels of Learnables Spanish, I recommend you move on to a second course: *Pimsleur Spanish*. The Pimsleur course begins your spoken practice (the next logical step). It is like having a private native-speaker tutor engaging you in real conversation. There are no textbooks, workbooks, nor any notes to take. Nothing to do but listen and talk. This is the *Rolls Royce* of language-learning courses. It is worth every penny it costs. At the successful completion of all three levels, you will be at the intermediate-high spoken level.

When we came to Mexico for our fact-finding mission, we decided to enroll in a language school--I had had *some* Spanish. In 1970 and 1975, I had studied Spanish. All I could say in the language was, "Hi!", "Where's the bathroom?", and "Can I have a cheese sandwich, please?" I was Spanish-challenged! I bought the courses I have mentioned here and went through them before coming for our fact-finding mission. When we arrived in Mexico in February 2003 for our fact-finding trip, and enrolled in a language school, I tested at the intermediate-high level.

These two systems work! If I were a zillionaire, I would buy these up and give them out as Christmas presents. That is just how sold I am on these two products. And, remember, I don't get one thin dime for promoting these language-learning courses. That they work is my motivation for recommending them to you!

I want to mention a word of warning before going on. Many Americans I've recommended these courses to will fall into a terrible habit. They have this irresistible urge to whip out pen and paper and start taking notes and making flash cards while using these two courses. *Do not do it!* No matter how strong the urge or temptation: *Don't do it!*

This note-taking and flash card business is so typical of college-educated Americans and especially those with law degrees! They can't get it out of their heads that learning spoken fluency in a second language is not like learning math or case law! These language courses plainly stress that note taking will short-circuit the language learning process. The place for note-taking and flash card making is when you are ready to climb on the *cart* (a formal grammar course). Do not do it while you are still on the *horse* stage of learning spoken fluency.

Follow the instructions exactly in both the Learnables and Pimsleur language courses. Do not deviate. Do not add to or subtract from the instructions. Once you've finished both courses, you will then be ready to graduate to a formal grammar course and then you can take all the notes you want and make a million flash cards if you wish. But not before then! Successfully ride the *horse* before hitching it up to the *cart* and letting it pull you along. The horse pulls the cart. Don't forget this!

Once you are in Mexico, whether visiting, on a fact-finding mission, or expatriating here, most cities will have language schools of varying degrees of quality. You will now be ready for a class or two after you've completed your spoken fluency program.

The whole issue here is to spend your money on something that works. You could spend a fortune on grammar classes that are by design not able to give you any ability to speak the language. What sense does that make? Or, you could spend your money on something that works: The Learnables and Pimsleur Spanish. These programs worked for me. They did what their literature promised they would do.

I've seen so many gringos come to Guanajuato, from America, who have taken years of traditional language courses and can't speak a word of Spanish. Or, their accent is so poor that they can't be understood. What's the point of that? These are people who have put the cart before the horse in their language learning process. Don't be one of them!

Chapter Eleven
Customs and Culture

When we moved to Mexico, the issue that troubled us most was accidentally making some cultural blunder. We were afraid we would do something to offend everyone we met. You can only read so much material on culture. What if you do something your research material did not cover? You don't want to offend the people you hope will let you live among them.

I think we are over this worry after living here for a while. We managed to learn some cultural guidelines that can steer a fledgling expatriate in the right direction. You will find some exceptions to these generalizations. Some of the younger-generation Mexicans ignore some of these old-time cultural principles while the traditionalists do not. My wife and I prefer the traditionalists' position on customs and culture.

You will notice that Mexicans are a kissing bunch of people. You will see this most often when they greet each other and when saying goodbye. At first, we were unsure how to handle this custom. Just who kisses and who does not? What is the rule if one exists?

When meeting a man or woman for the first time, you shake hands. Just as it used to be in the United States, you shake hands with a woman if she offers her hand to you first. Otherwise, you bow slightly and say, "Pleased to meet you".

The greeting kiss comes when *good* friends greet each other or say goodbye. Women will kiss women, men and women will kiss, but men rarely kiss other men. People kiss each other on the cheek or press their cheeks together and kiss the air. What defines *good* friends is open for debate.

I have been in circumstances where women have kissed me on the first introduction. I have shaken hands on the first introduction then we kiss on every other meeting. So, does that mean I became a *good* friend sometime between the first and second meetings? I don't know. As a male, I *never* initiate the kiss unless the woman is an old friend.

Men, thankfully, do not kiss each another. *Good* friends hug each other. Acquaintances shake hands. Let your Mexican friend or acquaintance initiate the contact.

Do not use first names with Mexicans until you are asked to do so. When we began renting our present home, we used the formal "usted" with our landlady and called her "Señora *(her last name)*" when addressing her. After a month or so, she insisted that we call her by her first name and that we use the informal "tu" when addressing her. Wait for others to give you permission to call them by their first names and use the "tu" form to address them.

There are people with whom you will probably never be on a first name basis and with whom you will always use the formal "usted". Our landlady's son, a dentist, is always referred to as "Doctor". He lives right next door to us, is our age or a bit younger, and uses the "tu" form when addressing each of us. However, he has not given us permission to use the "tu" form with him. Therefore, we call him "Doctor" and use the "usted" form.

Interestingly, our landlady's daughters-in-law always call her "Doña *(her first name)*" and use the formal "usted" with her.

If a person has a bachelor's degree from a university, you address him or her as "Licenciado" or "Licenciada" and then the last name. However, if a person is a doctor, lawyer, architect, teacher, or professor, you address him or her by title (Doctor, Abogado, Arquitecto, Maestro, or Professor) and last name. In the Mexican social hierarchy, these people have high rank and you are to afford them with much respect. In addition, plumbers, carpenters, electricians, and those in other professions requiring much training and skill are addressed as "Maestro" followed by the last name.

When someone invites you to a party or other event, shake the hand of each person (or kiss those who are good friends). Do this as well when you leave. If you neglect to do this, you will offend those whom you do not personally greet.

After getting past the greeting stage of an encounter, you want to be careful not to commit conversational boo-boos. Do not use the word "Indio" (Indian). It is derogatory. Do not ask a person what percentage of Indian blood he has. Mexicans are proud of their country's Indian heritage, but they consider the indigenous people beneath them and only claim pure Spanish blood.

Do not criticize the Mexican government. In fact, Mexicans consider it rude if you criticize your own government. They will not hesitate to criticize their government, but will take offense if you do it. Do not discuss the illegal alien issue in the United States.

If you see a Mexican male holding the arm of another male while the two are conversing, don't take offense. A man may touch another man on the arm or shoulder as an expression of close friendship. Don't recoil from the contact. To do so would be offensive. Shed your silly American connotations of male-to-male touching and realize that men can express affection for each other without any sexual overtones.

Women also touch each other often when talking or walking together. We have seen many women and girls walking arm-in-arm, walking with their arms around each other's shoulders, and even walking hand-in-hand. There is nothing sexual in these gestures. They are merely expressions of friendship.

When Mexicans meet on the street and stop to have a conversation, you will notice that they stand close to each other. Americans are protective of their personal space and want to put some distance between themselves and others. If you meet a Mexican friend or acquaintance on the street and stop for a conversation, don't back away when the other person stands closer than you like. To back away would give the impression that you don't want to be close to your friend and would be offensive.

If you ask a Mexican, "How's it going?" and it has not been going well, he will not answer, "Fine, thanks!" as we Americans are programmed to do. Instead, he will tell you that events in his life are not fine and will give you the details. Mexicans in general don't hide their feelings as Americans do. Mexicans regard Americans who hide their feelings as uncaring. Perhaps if Americans would assimilate this custom, they could decrease their Prozac and psychiatrist bills.

For the first few weeks in our new neighborhood, we would hear a hissing noise every time we walked down a certain section of the street. We would stop, look around, but see nothing. Finally, we noticed the door of one house was standing open. It was dark inside so we couldn't see anything. Suddenly, an older woman popped out, hissing and gesturing for us to come over. She had seen us walking by several times and wanted to meet us. This hissing noise is a common way to get someone's attention and is not rude.

Another public behavior that is normal here would cause a fistfight (or worse!) if tried in the United States. Whenever you stand in line for anything, don't be surprised if people push past you to be waited on first. Some will even interrupt you when you are giving your order to the shopkeeper. In the beginning, we thought that people were doing this because we were gringos. After a while, we began noticing that Mexicans practice this behavior toward other Mexicans. Finally, we asked our favorite shopkeeper why some people pushed in front of us in line and even interrupted our transactions. She said that it was because these people are rude and poorly educated in manners and not because we are gringos.

You will see this behavior often at the bus stops. There you are, waiting for your bus with nary a person in sight. Your bus appears down the street, so you move forward to the curb to await its arrival. Suddenly, a horde of people appears from nowhere! They push in front of you and even knock you aside to get on the bus first! You need to prepare for this behavior or the crowd will push you aside and you will miss your bus.

Apparently, standing in line is not a "Mexican" thing for many people. Traditionally, shopkeepers waited on those of high social rank or those who were older than anyone else in the store first. Some people hold to this tradition and some believe that "first come, first served" applies. We defer to the elderly, allowing someone with only one or two items to go ahead of us in the supermarket line, and allow women carrying babies to enter the bus in front of us. However, we have learned to push politely to the counter or to the bus door just as the Mexicans do.

When you are at the store or in a restaurant and you are ready to pay, be sure to place the money in the hand of the person you are paying. Do not place the money on the counter or on the table—you will give the impression that you are trying to avoid contact with the person. He will take offense and think you consider yourself to be better than he is. This may seem like a small detail, but it could help correct the Mexican conception that Americans are cold and standoffish.

There are actions that you should *not* do with your hands when you are in public. My favorite one is that men should *not* walk around with their hands in their pockets. It doesn't take much imagination to figure this one out!

Another custom is to keep both hands above the table while eating. You will have to overcome the American custom of keeping one hand in your lap while eating with the other. I'm not sure if many Mexicans know why this tradition began (if everyone could see both hands of everyone else at the table, no one could pull out a gun and shoot), but most follow it. Also, never put your elbows on the table while eating—it is rude in Mexico as well as in the United States.

Do not use the "come here" gesture Americans use— closed hand extended with the index finger curling back

and forth toward your body. Do not use the "OK" gesture—
making a circle with the thumb and index finger. These are
both obscene gestures in Mexico.

There are few, if any, public restrooms. You may find one
in a department store or a market, but you will have to pay
two or three pesos to use it. For your money, you will
receive a small piece of toilet paper—usually inadequate for
the job. We always carry some tissue or toilet paper with us.
Be prepared—many of the toilets do not have seats. Also,
you may want to carry some hand disinfectant (the kind you
rub on which doesn't require water) as sometimes the sinks
don't work. Most restrooms are spotlessly clean, but you
may find some that look as though they have never been
cleaned.

If you want to photograph someone in public, always ask
permission first. Offer to pay a nominal fee. Alternatively, if
you have a camera that prints an instant picture, offer to
give them a print. Some indigenous people do not like you
to photograph them. Some feel this is exploitation; some
think the photography process will steal their souls.

Trying to figure out what to wear in Mexico can be tricky.
Of course, you have to take the weather into consideration—
you don't need to bring your winter coat to Puerto Vallarta,
for instance. You also have to keep in mind how
conservative the city is.

In resort cities, it is common to see people wearing shorts
in public. In other cities, wearing shorts in public is rude.
Look at what Mexicans around your age are wearing and
follow suit.

Mexicans dress more conservatively than many
Americans do. You see more men wearing long pants than
shorts in public. Most women wear dresses or skirts, but
slacks and jeans are becoming more common. However, we
see more men and women wearing shorts now than we did

two years ago. However, do not wear shorts to fine restaurants, to church (even when you are just sightseeing), to the theater, or to someone's home.

Mexicans will dress up even to go shopping or to sit in the park. They are clean, their clothes neatly pressed, and their hair nicely arranged. Mexicans take offense at people who appear in public dressed shabbily or who are dirty.

If you experience the rare honor of an invitation to someone's home, dress casually but neatly. Men should wear a nice shirt and slacks; women should wear a dress, a skirt and blouse, or a pantsuit. If you are in doubt about the required attire, ask your host or hostess. We have been to parties where nearly everyone dressed in jeans and attractive shirts and blouses. We have also been to parties where everyone is more formally dressed.

Traditional Mexican meals and the times they are eaten take some getting used to. Breakfast can be any time between 6 and 11:30 a.m. and will usually be something light—juice or fruit, coffee, cereal or a pastry. Lunch, the day's largest meal, will be between 1:30 and 4:00 p.m. It usually consists of several courses beginning with soup. A rice or pasta dish or a salad may be a separate course or may accompany the main course. A pork chop, a piece of chicken or some enchiladas, vegetables, beans, tortillas or rolls make up the main course. A dessert (postre) rounds off the meal. Dinner will be around 8 p.m. and is something light. A small portion of the main dish from lunch, a couple of enchiladas or tacos, or a pastry is typical.

If you are having a meal at someone's home, there may be drinks and appetizers before the meal. When everyone has a drink, it is customary for all to raise their glasses and toast one another by saying, "Salud" (to your health). Once everyone sits at the table for the meal, it is customary to wish one another "Buen Provecho" (good appetite.)

The hostess will expect you to try everything served. She will offer you seconds, thirds, and even fourths if you clean your plate. If you don't like a particular dish or if something is too spicy for your taste, don't say anything; just leave most of it on your plate. Otherwise, the hostess will give you another serving. Do accept seconds on the dishes you like and be sure to compliment the hostess.

Sometimes, someone arranges the food on the plates in the kitchen. Sometimes, the hostess places bowls and platters of everything on the table to be passed family style. If the food is buffet style, wait to be asked before serving yourself. The hostess will encourage you to have seconds and will worry about you if you don't eat enough to meet her expectations.

Remember Mexicans invite only close friends and family to their homes. Remembering that, let humility, and politeness govern your actions. Always compliment the host and hostess on their home and compliment the hostess on the food and her cooking (even if she has a maid or cook who prepared the meal).

When to leave after the meal or party can be a little tricky. Take your cue from other guests. The host will not ask you to leave even if he is tired and wants you to go home. To do so would cause him to "lose face". Watch for signs that your hosts are tiring and take your leave, even if they insist that you stay longer. Be gracious and do not overstay your welcome.

If you are an overnight guest in a Mexican home, there are certain customs you should know. These will help make your stay enjoyable—not only for you, but also for your hosts.

Maintain an air of formality with your hosts. Use the formal "usted" until your hosts invite you to use the informal "tu" with them. Don't walk partially clothed or unclothed to the bathroom, put your feet on the furniture, or walk around shoeless in the house.

Be sure to find out mealtimes and observe them. Try to eat a meal out occasionally to ease the burden on your hosts—just be sure to tell them ahead of time so they don't make extra food or wait for you to show up before starting the meal. Take the family out for a meal or two as a gracious way of thanking them for their hospitality.

Offer to help with the dishes, cooking, or cleaning. Your hosts will likely not allow you to do any housework, but will appreciate your offer.

If your hosts have a maid who cleans your room and bathroom, leave her the peso equivalent of a few dollars each week of your stay. If the maid also does your laundry, you should tip her the peso equivalent of two or three dollars each time. Ask your hosts (or another Mexican friend) how much you should tip. Your hosts may tell you not to give the maid a tip, but you should do it anyway.

Begin and end your stay with small gifts for each family member. Mexicans like items that are unique to your area of the United States. They also appreciate pictures of your hometown and family. Children like music CDs and T-shirts. At the end of your stay, you will know your hosts' preferences, so you can give an appropriate gift—candy, perfume, a bottle of aged tequila.

You can never show too much gracious humility in each social encounter. Mexicans have had to endure brash, pushy, loud, rude Americans. Do your part to change their impression of Americans by practicing the suggestions in this chapter.

Chapter Twelve
What Do I Do With Myself?

After we answer the questions *why* and *how* we managed to move to Guanajuato, we are often asked, "What do you do with your time?" It is interesting that Europeans *never* ask us this question—only Americans and Canadians. I find this interesting and significant.

We usually respond to that question with a brief outline of a typical day's activities. We get up around 7:30 and eat breakfast on the patio with our parakeets. We putter around the house for a bit, shower, then head downtown. Sometimes we eat lunch at home before going out; sometimes we eat in one of our favorite restaurants. We might take in a movie or just relax in the park and practice our Spanish. Usually, we stop at a store or market for a few items, and then take the bus home. The rest of the day, we read and do some writing.

"I would have to do something *real* with my time", is the usual response by Americans to our daily routine. They seem repulsed at the thought of spending time "just" relaxing. Relaxation is a forgotten idea in the United States.

It is a small wonder why Americans are dropping dead from stress-related illnesses. Americans seem to have lost the ability to reduce stress, to practice relaxation, and to engage in endeavors that do not heighten their social or financial status.

A few years ago, as previously mentioned, I decided I wanted to learn Koine Greek, the original language of the Bible's New Testament. When I shared this wish with a family member, her response was, "That's great! What will you be able to do with that?"

Do you understand what she meant by that? She wanted to know how I would be able to earn more money in my job because of learning Koine Greek. I told her that I wanted to learn the language for the simple soul-satisfying pleasure of learning something new. I did not do it for any future monetary gains. She shook her head and looked confused.

It is the American mind-set that learning something to enrich one's mind is absurd. Knowledge and study are not good unless they will earn you more money or prestige. In fact, 68% of Americans who attend college state their *primary* reason as increasing their future earning power.

Here is what bothers me: of the college-bound age group (ages 18-24), 85% *cannot* find Iraq or Israel on an unmarked world map! Eighty-three percent *cannot* find Afghanistan, 58% *cannot* find Japan. Sixty-five percent *cannot* find France and 69% *cannot* find the United Kingdom.

Correct me if I am wrong, but aren't these people old enough to vote? And aren't many of these people marching in the streets against every conservative's efforts to combat terrorism in areas of the world they cannot *find* on a map? If they cannot find these countries on a map, do they even know much about the countries, their religion, and even what the issues are? I wonder.

Here in Guanajuato, the average citizen has more knowledge of American and world geography than many Americans have. Indeed, they have more knowledge of current events, American government and politics, and world issues than many college-educated Americans do. They know far more about America than Americans know about Mexico.

All of that to say this: my wife and I do take a break from our boring lives of relaxing, walking, reading, and writing to do something *real*. Guanajuato is packed with all sorts of *real* things to do and see.

The Alhondiga de Granaditas is a dreary-looking gray stone building, originally built for grain storage. During the struggle for independence from Spain, it served as a temporary fortress for the Spanish overlords. During the rule of Emperor Maximilian, an Austrian archduke appointed by Napoleon to govern Mexico, it served as a jail. Today, it is a museum of local history and art. On the four outside corners of the building, you can still see the hooks where the Spanish hung cages containing the heads of four leaders who led the rebel army during the struggle for independence.

La Basilica Colegiata de Nuestra Señora de Guanajuato is a monolithic, 17th-century church on the Plaza de la Paz. This Baroque church, painted yellowish-orange, houses one of the oldest Catholic icons in Mexico. Legend says the 8th-century wooden statue of the Virgin, given to Guanajuato in 1557 by King Philip II of Spain, was hidden in caves in Spain for centuries to keep it out of the hands of the Moors. The church also houses relics of St. Faustino the Martyr, which were presented to the church by the first Count of

Valenciana.

The Basilica is magnificent and well worth the time and effort to visit. As this is the parish church for the city, be aware there are frequent services. Therefore, show respect for the worshippers by not taking pictures, talking loudly or walking close to the altar during the service.

This is also a favorite location for weddings, especially on Saturdays. We have seen brides and wedding parties lined up in front of the church waiting for their turns—as many as four in an hour's time! Again, show respect for the wedding parties just as you would for worshippers.

Tucked on the left (north) side of the church is the Marian Gallery. Five rooms, dedicated to the Virgin Mary, display paintings and liturgical objects. The gallery's main purpose is the display and study of the image of Our Lady of Guanajuato.

The Jardin de la Union is one of the many plazas in Guanajuato. It is a small, triangular park across the street from Teatro Juarez in the downtown area. Huge Indian laurel trees and benches line the walkway and enclose a bandstand (the site of frequent concerts), fountains, and flowerbeds. Restaurants, hotels, and shops surround the plaza. The Jardin is the place to see and be seen. As a result, it is always an interesting place to have a meal or drink, eat an ice-cream cone, practice your Spanish or just relax.

Teatro Juarez is an impressive piece of architecture, both inside and out. Statues of eight Greek Muses line the roof and large stone lions flank the steps. The inside is Moorish in décor and is elegant. One visitor said that being inside the theater was like being inside an exquisite music box. The theater is the site for frequent plays, operas, and concerts. The steps in front are the site for many impromptu performances by clowns, mimes, jugglers, and troubadours. You can take a tour of the interior for a few pesos on days when no performance is scheduled.

If your taste runs to the macabre, you can visit the famous Mummy Museum and its accompanying "Cult of Death" display. I have to tell you—this is the most horrific museum I have ever seen! School-age kids love touring the museum regularly. Once was more than enough for us!

These mummies are not like the Egyptian mummies you may have seen in museums. The Egyptians intentionally mummified their dead and, thankfully, wrapped the mummies in cloth. The Guanajuato mummies were not mummified on purpose nor were they wrapped in cloth.

Guanajuato's soil, rich in lime and clay, dehydrates tissue and prevents decomposition. Also, the area is dry, which aids the mummification.

In 1853, the city began building a city cemetery to bury the dead. By 1896, the cemetery became crowded because there was a change in the law dealing with payments for the plots. If a family could not pay the yearly fee for the plot, then the city exhumed the family's dearly departed relatives to make room for newer arrivals. A little gruesome, isn't it?

When the workers exhumed the bodies, they noticed many of the bodies were mummified and were in good shape. Not knowing what to do with these mummies, they propped them up around the fence surrounding the cemetery. Just think about seeing that sight when going to pay your respects to your dead relatives! To make matters worse, the propped-up mummies would occasionally fall over on the visitors!

City officials finally decided to put the best-looking mummies on display in a museum and to charge admission. There are over 100 mummies on display, some still wearing their burial clothes. The city reported recently the museum makes more than $800,000 pesos yearly in admissions and souvenir sales.

If shopping is more to your taste, then a visit to Mercado Hidalgo is order. This is an indoor market, housed in a huge two-story building that looks more like a train station or airplane hanger than a market.

Rows and rows of stalls cover the first floor and sell a huge variety of produce, meat, grocery items, pet supplies, household items, candy, and more. There are also a few lunch counters where you can have a snack, a meal, or just a soft drink.

The second floor is just a narrow balcony along the walls with some stalls selling various items appealing to tourists. You will find pottery, blankets, t-shirts, sombreros, postcards, and more. This level provides an overview of the first floor stalls as well as an unobstructed view of the ceiling soaring above you.

Stalls are also set up around the outside of the building. Some sell produce, cheese, tortillas, or chocolate. Others sell odd assortments of items—baby clothes next to tools, CDs with hardware. You can find just about anything you need, short of furniture and kitchen appliances, inside and outside Mercado Hidalgo. It is always crowded and has a carnival-type atmosphere with each vendor shouting for you to choose from his products.

The Pipila Monument is another interesting site to visit in Guanajuato. Dedicated to Juan Jose de los Reyes Martinez, an important figure in Mexico's fight for independence, it overlooks the city and provides an incredible view. If you have the time and a stout heart, you can make the 30-minute climb to the statue via a callejon (alley) from the downtown area. Otherwise, take a city bus marked, "Pipila", take a cab, or take the funicular behind Teatro Juarez.

The 272-year-old University of Guanajuato can offer many wonderful diversions. This former Jesuit seminary offers outstanding educational opportunities as well as a total Spanish immersion program for foreign students. In addition, the tuition is very reasonable.

The main building looks more like a medieval castle than a school. It has an enormous, steep stairway that seems to reach into the heavens. Climbing it is a feat of which to be proud! We still haven't made it to the top (I would have to be airlifted to the nearest hospital if I tried it at this point!), but one day we will.

Guanajuato formerly supplied the world with one-third of its silver. Valenciana, a suburb-like community north of the city, has a functioning silver mine that opened in 1529 and was one of the richest in the world. An interesting guided tour is available where you can learn the mine's history.

Near the mine is a famous 18th-century colonial church. It has hand-carved and gilded wooden altars as well as many impressive paintings. The first Count of Valenciana financed the building of the church in thanks to God for the rich silver strike at his mine. This is well worth the time and effort to visit. You can take a cab from Guanajuato for around 30 pesos (about $3.00 USD) or a bus marked, "Valenciana" from a stop near the Alhondiga de Granaditas.

While in Valenciana, you can visit several interesting shops filled with pottery, clothing, and artwork from Guanajuato, Michoacan, Oaxaca, and other parts of Mexico. In addition, you can eat at a fine restaurant called "Casa del Conde de la Valenciana".

If you want to become an active participant in the life of the city, you can volunteer in some of the local charitable organizations. Some were formed by gringos to aid local children, increase literacy, and help needy families. All the major "Gringo Land" cities have these sorts of charitable groups.

If you are a traveler, there is an entire country to visit. Bus fares are reasonable. You can use one town as your home base and travel around the region or country. We have met many expatriates who have done this.

Another source of cheap entertainment is eating in restaurants. You will find that your Mexican friends will be more likely to invite you to share a meal in a restaurant than in their homes. We have been invited to Mexicans' homes for meals on occasion, but have found that entertaining in restaurants is more common.

On a recent trip to the United States, we decided to have lunch at a popular cafeteria. We loved to eat at this particular chain when we lived in the States and looked forward to eating some of our old favorites.

We both ordered chicken fried steak, mashed potatoes with cream gravy, two vegetables, a bread item, tea, and dessert. There were two items we had forgotten about the American restaurant dining experience: the price and the portion size. This was lunch in a *cafeteria* not a five-star restaurant! We had to pay $25 for an ordinary meal that we had to carry to a table on a plastic tray!

The portion sizes surprised us as well. Between us, we had enough food to feed four people and these were regular portions, not double ones! We could not begin to finish everything on our plates, but ate more than we wanted out of guilt. We returned to our motel room, found the antacid tablets, and tried to calm our beleaguered stomachs for the rest of the afternoon.

When we eat out in Mexico, we try to go for lunch after 1:30 or so. This is because most restaurants offer an inexpensive set meal of the day during this time. The choices vary from day to day and offer a chance to try different foods prepared in several ways.

The meal of the day usually consists of a soup, rice or pasta, a main dish, a vegetable or salad, rolls or tortillas, and a dessert. Some restaurants include a drink (usually a nonalcoholic fruit drink) in the price of the meal. The price of this meal in Guanajuato varies from less than $3.00 to $8.00 or more.

Unlike the mega-portions found in many American restaurants, Mexican restaurants usually serve small but satisfactory servings. Unless you have a huge appetite, the meal of the day will fill you up without making you uncomfortable.

If you have a large appetite or the meal of the day doesn't appeal to you that day, you can order from the regular menu. You can order a good-sized steak, complete with salad, rice, French fries, and rolls for $6.00 or so.

You will find traditional Mexican foods on the menu, not what you may be familiar with at your favorite Mexican restaurant back home. Soups such as Sopa Azteca (Tortilla Soup) and Pozole (a hominy-based soup) are common. Chilis Rellenos (poblano chilies stuffed with various fillings, dipped in egg batter, and fried) are a traditional dish. Mole dishes (no, not "mole" as in the animal, but a spicy, semi-sweet chocolate sauce poured over meat) and enchiladas are also common menu items.

Guanajuato has a traditional dish called "Enchiladas Mineras". These are corn tortillas stuffed with chunks of potatoes and carrots (and sometimes chicken), cooked in a mild chili sauce, topped with lettuce, tomato, and crumbled soft cheese. They are usually served with a piece of chicken. Delicious!

If you are timid about using Spanish, Guanajuato has a few restaurants with bilingual menus and staff. For a very good meal (and generous portions), we recommend *Casa*

Valadez, located on the corner of the Jardin de la Union across from Teatro Juarez. The waiters are friendly and attentive. The restaurant serves an excellent bacon and mushroom cheeseburger with French fries if you feel the need for an American-style hamburger. They also serve *huge* tossed salads. These are a rarity in Mexico, where salads usually consist of a piece of lettuce, a few thin rings of onion, and a slice of tomato.

There are scores of small eateries hidden in nooks and crannies throughout Guanajuato. Most are small—only 3 or 4 tables—and serve a limited menu. Most are safe and economical choices for a meal or snack, but exercise caution.

These small mom-and-pop places are not always the cleanest places to eat. Sometimes, the restaurant is the front room of someone's home. The family decided they needed a few extra pesos this month, so they threw a couple of tables and some chairs in the living room, and, presto, you have a restaurant. Sometimes, the restaurant is on the patio or on the sidewalk in front of the house. These don't usually last for more than a few weeks and they don't have a reputation to protect, so watch out.

Look at the food preparation area if you are able. Is the food refrigerated or sitting out on a counter? Is there a sink (with hot water) for washing dishes or just a bucket of standing water? Does the person who cooks the food also handle the dirty dishes and the money? Any of these have the potential of making you very ill.

Having said that, I must tell you there are a few frightening-looking restaurants that have great food, good service, and are safe. A restaurant in this category is one that sells pollo asado (chicken roasted on giant rotisseries), usually located at the front of the restaurant. These are very popular and the chickens sell as fast as they finish roasting.

Guanajuato has one of these restaurants called "La

Carretera". It is an open-fronted restaurant with the oven right in front, almost on the sidewalk. You can order quarter, half or whole roasted chickens, to eat in or carry out, with generous sides of flavored rice, cole slaw, tortillas (made fresh in the kitchen), and all the jalapeños you can eat. A whole chicken with sides for two and two soft drinks costs less than $9.00.

Something disturbing about eating in restaurants in Mexico is that beggars and vendors will often accost you at your table. Some will even ask you for some of your food. However, try not to let them ruin your meal…this is just part of Mexican life.

Don't be afraid to try foods that are unfamiliar to you. Ask the waiter to describe the food (is it a fruit, a vegetable, a meat, what cut of meat, and so forth) and ask if it is "muy picante" or "un poco picante" (very spicy or a little spicy.) Trying new foods is part of the adventure of visiting or living in Mexico.

Mexican cities and towns teem with street vendors selling some of the most delicious-smelling foods you can imagine. Some sell food that has been cooked at home then brought to the park or market to sell. Some have rolling carts, complete with gas grills, where they cook the food in front of you. Some keep the uncooked foods in coolers filled with ice; some just have a pile of unrefrigerated meat on the counter.

These carts do not have running water, so the vendors have a couple of buckets of dubious-looking water (into which they often pour bleach) for washing and rinsing the dirty dishes. Avoid these at all costs! No matter how delicious the food looks, the dirty plates and utensils will surely do you in.

Foods to avoid are mayonnaise (unless someone has just opened the jar in front of your eyes), yogurt, and sour cream. Containers of these sit out in the hot sun all day without refrigeration. They are just waiting to slather on your ear of roasted corn or poured over your bowl of fresh fruit. Or, maybe smeared on your shredded pig jowl, lettuce, salsa-topped bag of potato chips (I'm not kidding!).

The moral of the story is: *never* eat off the street! Our Mexican friends say they never eat from street vendors, no matter how appetizing the food looks or how many other Mexicans are eating at a particular cart.

This also applies to shops that sell pizza by-the-slice. These pizzas often sit for hours under light bulbs and are almost guaranteed to make you ill. If you want a piece of pizza, go to a pizza restaurant where they will make you a fresh, hot pizza. It is safer.

You probably will not find a wide variety of ethnic restaurants if you choose a small Mexican city. Guanajuato has one Chinese and Japanese restaurant combination, a fast-food Japanese restaurant, a couple of Italian restaurants, and a couple of French restaurants. Larger cities and towns with many tourists will provide you more choices.

However, you will have plenty of restaurants from which to choose wherever you live (unless you live in a rural area or a village with a tiny population). You will be able to find restaurants to fit your budget as well as higher-priced restaurants when you want to splurge.

Be forewarned—American fast food chains are spreading in Mexico. When we moved to Guanajuato, the only chain was Domino's Pizza. It has now been joined by Dunkin' Donuts and Baskin-Robbins Ice Cream. Other cities have Pizza Hut, Kentucky Fried Chicken, Domino's, Burger King, McDonald's, Sirloin Stockade-you name it. All that you can think of that has helped create morbidly obese people in America can be found in larger Mexican cities.

Lastly, other ways to spend your time in Mexico are to

engage *seriously* in those hobbies that you never had time for in the States. Maybe you always wanted to paint or do photography. Maybe you have dreamed of making pottery or doing woodworking. We enjoy writing and raising exotic birds. Now that we have time, we are pursuing both of those hobbies. You will have time as well; so learn a new skill or resurrect an old one and enjoy!

Chapter Thirteen
Frequently Asked Questions

1. Q: Is learning Spanish difficult?

A: It depends on your motivation and the method you use to learn it. If you are highly motivated, use the methods I mentioned in Chapter Nine. You will advance rapidly.

2. Q: Is learning the peso-dollar exchange rates difficult?

A: Not at all. If an item costs 200 pesos, just divide by the current exchange rate to find out the amount in US Dollars. The rate has been over 11 pesos to the US Dollar for several months, so we just divide the number of pesos by 11 to calculate the amount in dollars. After a while, you will find that you stop comparing pesos to dollars and just think in pesos.

3. Q: Can a foreigner buy real estate in Mexico?

A: Yes, foreigners can buy real estate. However, the process is a bit different in Mexico than in the USA.

4. Q: Can I open a Mexican bank account?

A: Yes. You will need to ask the bank what documents they need. Some will only allow you to open an account if you have a valid FM-3 visa; some will open an account if you just have a tourist visa. You will also need to have a copy of your lease (if you rent) and current copies of utility bills showing your address (it doesn't matter if the name on the bill is your landlord's name and not your name). You will also need to have a minimum amount of pesos for your first deposit.

5. Q: Can I direct deposit my Social Security, disability or pension check into my Mexican account?

A: You may be able to do this, but check with the Social Security Administration (www.ssa.gov) or your pension company. Also, check with your Mexican bank to see if they can handle direct deposits from the United States.

You may want to have your check deposited into a U.S. bank and then withdraw a lump sum each month to deposit into your Mexican account to use as you need it. The value of the peso has changed over the years (sometimes a great deal) and your peso account could devalue overnight. Most experts recommend keeping most of your money in a U.S. bank and only transferring enough to your Mexican account to cover a month or two of expenses.

6.   Q: How can I avoid getting "la turista?"

A: "La turista", also known as "Montezuma's Revenge", refers to a gastrointestinal upset caused by bacteria. You can avoid it by practicing the suggestions we list in Chapter Fourteen. Drink only purified water (and use it to brush your teeth) and wash your hands often (especially before eating). Peel vegetables and fruits or soak them in a chlorine or iodine solution, and avoid foods that have been sitting out without refrigeration. Many travelers carry antibacterial hand cleaners to use when sinks are not available.

If you get a case of "la turista" despite taking proper precautions, drink plenty of clear liquids (chamomile tea is easy on the stomach). Avoid alcohol and dairy products for a few days. When you can keep liquids down, you can introduce plain gelatin, tortillas, and rice. If you cannot keep liquids down or if the diarrhea continues, see a doctor immediately. You may need an antibiotic as well as medication to slow down your gastrointestinal tract.

7.   Q: How can I check my e-mail?

A: Almost everywhere you go you will find Internet cafes. The computer age has come to Mexico, but most Mexicans cannot afford home computers or Internet connections. Therefore, Internet cafes have sprung up all over. For 8-15 pesos an hour, you can check your e-mail, surf the Internet, play computer games, or type papers.

8.   Q: How can I get around?

A: In Guanajuato, cab fares are around 25 pesos in town and around 35 pesos if you want to go to the bus station. If you call a cab, you will have to pay an additional 10 pesos. City buses cost 2 ½ pesos (about

$0.20 USD) and have routes all over town. Guanajuato is small enough that you can walk most places.

If you want to travel around Mexico, buses are very inexpensive and comfortable. The buses have air-conditioning, movies, and restrooms. Some have galleys where you can fix yourself a cup of coffee or hot tea and some even serve snacks.

9. Q: How can I get money in Mexico?

A: There are ATM machines in most cities where you can access your US (and Mexican) bank account. Some machines only dispense pesos; some give you a choice between pesos and dollars. Usually, the ATM will give you a better exchange rate than a bank or a currency exchange office. If you have traveler's checks, banks and some hotels will cash them into pesos for you, but you need to show your passport. If you have cash in dollars, you will have to exchange them for pesos at a currency exchange office (unless you are in certain resorts cities or border towns where dollars are accepted). You can also get a cash advance on your credit card at ATMs or banks.

10. Q: How can I avoid being a crime victim?

A: Take the same precautions you would if you visited Los Angeles, Detroit, Chicago, New York City or Miami. Avoid wearing expensive jewelry, don't flash large amounts of cash in public, don't leave cameras and other attractive items in your car in plain view, and be aware of your surroundings.

11. Q: What if I am disabled?

A: In Guanajuato, there are few concessions for the disabled. Some downtown streets and sidewalks have wheelchair ramps, but not many of the surrounding areas do. Guanajuato has many steep streets and many steps, so wheelchair navigation is difficult. Also, since many buildings are constructed on the sides of mountains, houses and hotels can have many steps (and few elevators). However, we have seen an increasing number of people in wheelchairs or using walkers and canes, so it is possible to get around.

Newer resort hotels provide more accommodations for the disabled than many of the older hotels in the country. These have elevators and wheelchair ramps and may have rooms with extra-wide doorways, roll-in showers, and grab bars.

12.   Q: Will I need a passport?

A: If you are visiting on a tourist visa and only plan to stay in Mexico for a short time, you will need an original birth certificate, but not a passport. However, if you plan to use traveler's checks or if you plan to move to Mexico, you will need a US passport.

The U.S. State Department recently changed the requirements for Americans returning to the States after visiting Mexico, Latin America, and the Caribbean. Now, they require travelers to have a valid passport or other acceptable documentation to enter the United States. You may want to check with your airline or the State Department before your trip to find out what their requirements are then.

13. Q: How do I find public restrooms?

A: There are public restrooms in Mexico, but they are not as plentiful as in the United States. Large department stores and supermarkets have them, but you may need to pay a few pesos to use them. Restaurants and movie theaters have restrooms, but you can only use them if you are eating a meal or attending a movie.

You can find a few public restrooms close to parks, in bus stations, and in some of the markets. You will be charged a few pesos for the privilege of using them. Be sure to carry some tissues with you as your pesos will only buy you a small piece of toilet paper. Also, it is a good idea to carry a small bottle of hand sanitizer with you since sometimes, there are no paper towels available and sometimes there is no water. Some of these restrooms are clean, others are not, and many have no toilet seats.

14.   Q: How should I behave while visiting Mexico?

A: If you read Chapter Two, you know inappropriate behavior in public is one of our pet peeves. Rudeness, obscenities, and rage behavior are not the way to act in any country. Instead, be polite, kind, patient, humble, and treat others the way you would like to be treated. Remember that you are in Mexico where things don't always work the way you are used to in the United States. Remember that you are a guest in Mexico and behave as you would as a guest in someone's home.

15. Q: Should I use traveler's checks?

A: Traveler's checks from a well-known international company like American Express, Visa, or MasterCard are the most familiar and therefore the easiest to cash. You will need to exchange your traveler's checks for pesos at a bank or currency exchange office since most stores and restaurants will not accept them as payment. Some of the more expensive hotels may cash them for you, but you may not get as good an exchange rate as a bank would give you.

16. Q: Can a woman safely travel alone in Mexico?

A: Yes. However, you must be prepared to deal with much male attention including catcalls and whistles on the streets. Be cautious and travel with a group, especially at night. Also, be aware that many bars, especially cantinas, are for males only...women are not welcome. If you want to go to a bar or nightclub with a group of women, ask your hotel manager to recommend a suitable place.

17. Q: How much should I tip for various services?

A: You are not required to tip taxi drivers unless they help you with your luggage (though we give them a small tip anyway). Waiters should receive 10% of the total bill (more if the service was excellent). The same goes for the barber or stylist who does your hair. You should tip your hotel maid the equivalent of a couple of dollars a day. If you take a guided tour, you should tip the guide 10% of the cost of the tour.

18. Q: Can I use my electrical appliances in Mexico?

A: The electric current is the same in Mexico as in the United States. However, many older houses and hotels do not have grounded outlets that accommodate 3-prong plugs. If your razor, clock, or hair dryer has a 3-prong plug, you should bring an adaptor for it.

There are frequent voltage surges, brownouts, and occasional power outages, so you should bring a surge protector and maybe a voltage regulator as well to protect your stereo and television. Also, it would be a good idea to bring a voltage regulator with a battery backup if you want to use your laptop or desktop computer.

19. Q: Are vaccinations necessary?

A: We have met many Europeans, both students and tourists, who got all manner of immunizations before they left home and became ill anyway. Our U.S. doctor told us that no special immunizations were necessary for central Mexico, but we would need vaccinations for various tropical diseases if we planned on spending any time in the tropics. Check the Centers for Disease Control and Prevention website for information on destinations, vaccinations, diseases, and more.

20. Q: Can I work in Mexico?

A: Maybe. To work in Mexico, you must provide a service that no Mexican in that area can adequately perform. In addition, you must have a work visa allowing a specific company to employ you. If you change companies, you must get a new visa for the new company.

Teaching English is a possibility if you are a native English speaker. Schools, both public and private, are almost always in need of native English speakers. They may have Mexican teachers who can teach English, but want to use native speakers whenever possible.

Don't expect to strike it rich teaching English in Mexico. You may be offered as much as $12 an hour in Mexico City, but the norm throughout the rest of Mexico is between $3 and $6 an hour. If a large school hires you, they may offer you full-time work. If, however, a small school hires you, they may only offer you 10 or so hours a week. We have met several English teachers who have to teach at 3 or more different schools to make a modest living.

21. Q: What should I pack for my trip?

A: Check out The Weather Channel website, type in the name of the city or cities you plan to visit, and click on averages and records. There is a chart which gives you the average monthly highs, lows, and rainfall. You can also look at the current forecast. This will give you an idea about the clothing you will need.

If you are planning to visit areas at high elevations, you will need to bring a sweater or light jacket for the evenings, even during the summer. During the winter months, you should bring a heavier jacket, a sweater, and a warm hat. You won't need these during the day, but it can get chilly after the sun goes down. Also, you should bring something warm to sleep in (like sweats or flannel pajamas) since most hotels do not have central heat.

If you are planning to visit tropical areas, bring light clothes that breathe well (like cotton). Jeans and shirts that contain polyester are just too warm and don't allow perspiration to evaporate. In these areas, you will need a hat that gives you complete coverage and good shade as well as sunscreen with a high SPF rating.

Of course, you should bring clothing suitable for whatever activities you are planning to pursue. Bring bathing suits for the beach and boots for hiking. If you want to snorkel or scuba dive, you don't need to bring your equipment with you (unless you are driving and have room to spare) since you can rent whatever you need here.

Another important item to pack is a good, comfortable pair of walking shoes that give you proper support. For the cobblestone streets and sidewalks of central Mexico, we find that All-Terrain walking or running shoes give us the best support.

You should bring an umbrella and light raincoat even if your visit is not scheduled during the region's rainy season. It can rain any time of the year and the downpours can be very heavy, especially in the tropics.

It is easy to find a place to have your laundry done for you, so you don't need to pack enough clothes for the entire trip. Your hotel may have laundry facilities or a laundry service.

If you are flying or taking the bus, you should pack a change of clothes in your carry-on bag. All your medications, essential toiletries, and pertinent papers should be packed in your carry-on luggage in case the rest of your luggage is lost or delayed.

I just want to give a word of advice about toiletries. You will be able to find many American brands of makeup and other toiletries, but they are expensive. Mexican brands are just as effective and are less expensive. However, you should bring enough of your essentials to last a few days. Who wants to spend time looking for a drugstore immediately? Also, if you are visiting somewhere with an arid climate, moisturizer is a necessity. Even if you have oily skin, you will find your skin will be drier than normal. Also, you may want to switch to a moisturizing shampoo.

22. Q: How can I make phone calls?

A: If the housing you secure does not have a telephone, you can buy telephone debit cards to use at public pay phones. Many stores and markets sell these cards—look for a sign in the window or ask the shopkeeper.

These cards are easy to use, come in various denominations, and can be used to make local as well as long-distance calls. The telephones have computer screens which show you how much credit remains on your card. Most telephone booths have detailed instructions on how to make international calls.

23. Q: What can I bring into Mexico?

A: If you enter on a tourist visa, you can bring a camera, some film, a few CDs, a laptop computer, medications (in their original bottles and accompanied by written prescriptions from your doctor), toiletries, and clothing. Access the U.S. State Department website, click on "Regional Information" under "Tips for Traveling Abroad" on the left side of the page, and then click on "Tips for Travelers to Mexico" for a complete list.

If you get an FM-3 visa, you have 3 months to bring a "reasonable" amount of household items into Mexico without paying duty. You can find a list of customs rules at the Mexico International Movers website. Click on "Customs Regulations" under "Quick Links" and then click on "International Movers Mexico". You will find a list of required documents, items on which you will have to pay duty, forbidden items, information on how to import your car, truck, or boat, and how to bring in your pet. You can also get an estimate of the cost of moving your household items on this website.

24. Q: I don't speak Spanish. Who could I contact in Mexico for assistance?

A: In regions where there is a large English-speaking population, you will have little difficulty finding someone to help you. If you are in a more traditional Mexican town, you may have some trouble finding people who speak English. The tourist office may have someone who speaks English or will know someone who does. You can also go to any of the language schools that teach Spanish to foreigners—there will be English speakers there who can help you.

25. Q: As a senior citizen on a limited income, how would I go about finding an economical community to live in if I want to stay in Mexico?

A: Depending on your physical condition, you could live in one of the colonial cities like Guanajuato. However, if you don't speak Spanish or you have physical limitations, you might want to consider places where expatriates congregate-Lake Chapala, San Miguel de Allende or Puerto Vallarta. Some of these areas may not be as economical as smaller Mexican towns.

26. Q: How can I find a reputable doctor?

A: In small towns where there is not a large expatriate community, you might have difficulty finding a doctor who speaks English. If your Spanish is good, you won't have trouble finding a good doctor in any but the most rural areas of Mexico.

If you visit or live in a city with many expatriates, ask several people to recommend doctors that they like. You may find there are several English-speaking doctors from which to choose.

27. Q: If I have special needs, such as being on a low-fat or low-sugar diet, will I be able to find the products I need easily?

A: The low-fat, low-sugar craze has just appeared in Mexico recently. You will be able to find low-fat and fat-free milk and yogurt, though we have not found low-fat cheese in Guanajuato. There are several sugar substitutes, diet soft drinks, and fruit drinks made without sugar. You will not find as extensive a selection of low-fat, fat-free, and sugar-free products as you may be used to seeing in the United States, at least not in the smaller cities or towns. You are likely to find better selections in larger cities and places that have large numbers of expatriates.

28. Q: If the water is not safe to drink, what do you use for drinking and cooking water?

A: Most people use purified bottled water for drinking and cooking. Companies will deliver five-gallon bottles of water to your doorstep in most areas. You can also buy bottled water in most grocery stores.

Some people boil their water to kill the germs. We have read various opinions on the boiling time needed for the water to be safe; just until it reaches a rolling boil or maintaining a rolling boil for 10 to 40 minutes. We don't use this method because the water in Guanajuato contains minerals and we don't like the taste.

There are single-faucet and whole-house water filtration systems available. These filter out most of the bacteria and minerals. The single-faucet filters cost less than $50 and the filters, which last for six months, only cost about $10 each. This is the method we use. Whole-house filtration systems are more convenient, but also more costly both to install and maintain.

29. Q: What is the average cost of cab service?

A: In Guanajuato, cab fares within the city are 25 pesos (less than $2.25 USD) and around 35 pesos (around $3.10 USD) for most of the outlying areas. Prices vary from city to city, so ask the price before you jump in.

30. Q: How can I find out which places Americans should avoid in Mexico?

A: Remember the golden rule of safety: When in doubt, don't! Just like in your own city or state, exercise common sense. Avoid secluded ATMs, especially late at night. Don't walk down unfamiliar, deserted streets alone, especially at night. Ask your Mexican neighbors which areas to avoid.

For regions of Mexico to avoid, check the U.S. State Department website for current travel warnings.

31. Q: How can I meet new people and make new friends, both American and Mexican?

A: In areas that have large expatriate populations, you are just liable to have the Welcome Wagon at your door before you can unpack. These communities have many clubs and events where you can meet people.

In smaller towns where there is less of an expatriate presence, you won't find as many clubs or activities. However, you will see other expatriates on the streets, in the stores, and in the parks. Be brave and introduce yourself. They will likely know most, if not all, the other expatriates in town and can tell you about any clubs or events in which you involve yourself.

Making friends with your Mexican neighbors may be a bit more difficult. They will be polite toward you, but will be slow to warm up to you and become friends. It's not you-it's cultural. Be friendly, greet your neighbors whenever you see them on the street, ask about their families and eventually they will open up. Of course, you will have to speak some Spanish to accomplish this as many do not speak or understand much English. Be persistent--it is worth the effort!

32. Q: How long does it take to become a legal resident alien?

A: You can apply for legal resident status at a Mexican Consulate in the United States before you make the move. Use an Internet search engine to find a list of Mexican Consulate offices in the United States.

Some people recommend coming into Mexico for the first time on a tourist visa, then applying for resident status at a Mexican Immigration office once you decide that you want to live in Mexico. This is because a tourist visa is inexpensive (around $20 USD) and requires little paperwork. A resident visa is more costly and requires more paperwork.

33. Q: Are U.S. brands available in Mexico or will I have to buy only Mexican brands?

A: You will find a few U.S. brands in the supermarkets and places like Wal-Mart, Sam's Club, and Costco. Keep in mind the stores import most from the U.S. and they will be more expensive than they were back home. Mexican brands are just as good as U.S. brands and are much less expensive.

34. Q: Can I bring household electronics such as microwaves, televisions, and computers into Mexico?

A: If you come into Mexico on a tourist visa, you can bring a laptop computer in duty-free. However, you may not be able to bring in other electronics (or you may be required to pay a duty or import tax).

If you come in within 3 months of receiving your FM3 visa, you can bring in used (more than six months old) electronics. However, you must list the items with their serial numbers, date you bought them, cost, and descriptions on the required customs forms.

35. Q: What is the monthly cost for Internet service in my home?

A: Prodigy reigns here in Guanajuato, as well as in other regions of Mexico. A broadband, high-speed Internet connection will cost you around 400 pesos a month (about $36 USD). If you sign a 2-year contract, there is no installation charge. If you don't want to sign a long-term contract, there is an initial fee of 1000 pesos (about $89 USD).

There are also companies which provide dial-up service for about 189 pesos (about $17 USD) a month. These can become almost as expensive as broadband if you are not careful. Telmex, the Mexican telephone company, allows you 100 phone calls a month before they start charging you for each call. If you dial your service provider several times each day, get disconnected and have to reconnect (something that happens often), plus make regular phone calls, your charges can add up fast.

36. Q: Can a single person live comfortably on $1000 USD a month in Mexico?

A: Yes, depending on the region you choose and your lifestyle choices. An employee who works for minimum wage in Mexico earns around $400 USD a month. With $1000 a month, you will live well above that level.

37. Q: Are older people treated with respect in Mexico?

A: Our observation is that young people treat older people as important parts of the family and society. Older people are considered to be full of wisdom and knowledge, and as people who can contribute to those around them. Mexico has few, if any, nursing homes. Instead, the elderly live with children or grandchildren when they are not able to live independently.

38. Q: Do most homes have bathtubs as well as showers?

A: Most homes we have seen only have showers. A few have bathtubs, but they are the exception. Most of the houses and apartments advertised for sale or rent, at least in our area, say the bathrooms are equipped with showers.

39. Q: Is it safe to brush your teeth or shower using tap water?

A: We've heard both yes and no in response to this question. Some guidebooks say to brush your teeth only with bottled water and to keep your mouth shut while showering. Others say that brushing your teeth with tap water is fine as long as you don't swallow. I brush with tap water and have not experienced trouble. My wife only brushes with filtered water, but she has had more gastrointestinal problems than I have had. It is your choice on this one.

40. Q: Is the electrical service reliable or are there frequent power outages?

A: It is more or less reliable, though there are sometimes outages during thunderstorms or when there is high wind. Sometimes, though, there are outages for no obvious reason. We have noticed that power outages sometimes occur during large festivals that require huge amounts of electricity for lighting and sound. The power is rarely off for long, though. Five hours is the longest we have had to wait for it to be restored.

41. Q: Are there good markets in most neighborhoods or will I have to travel long distances to shop?

A: Guanajuato has small stores just about everywhere, so you won't have to walk far to get what you need. If you want a supermarket or a Wal-Mart SuperCenter, then you may have to take a bus or drive your car a long way to do your shopping.

42. Q: What is the most difficult thing, besides the language, to get used to in Mexico?

A: For us it was the noise level. It seems that Mexicans will have a party or celebration for any reason or for no reason. These parties have loud music and sometimes explosive charges (not just fireworks) that rattle windows. There is also a lot of singing, loud talking, and laughing. Sometimes, the celebrations start at dawn and last all day and into the night. All you can do is get some good earplugs and wait it out. Or, you can go join the party and have a good time.

43. Q: What can I expect my cost-of-living expenses to be?

A: As we wrote in Chapter Four, it is difficult to estimate costs since they are dependent on the region you choose and your lifestyle choices. That chapter gives you some estimates.

44. Q: How long will it take me to adjust to the culture?

A: Our opinion is the faster you learn enough Spanish to carry on simple conversations with your Mexican neighbors, the faster you will become comfortable in the culture. Also, if you can read the daily newspaper, you will find out what is going on in town. That will also help you adjust as well as tell you about events you can attend to get out into the community. In our view, not being able to ask questions (and understanding the responses!) about things you don't know or understand is the chief problem that causes culture shock.

45. Q: Do cities like Guadalajara and Guanajuato have direct airline service to the United States?

A: Yes, though you may have to make connections in the U.S. to get to your final destination.

46. Q: Do Mexican cities have a type of "9-1-1" emergency telephone number?

A: Yes. In Guanajuato, the number is "066". Check your city's telephone book for the number in your region.

47. Q: Is it safe to walk my dog in cities where there is a feral dog problem?

A: Usually, yes. If you have a small dog, you may have to hold it if you meet aggressive feral dogs. For all dogs, it is advisable to keep their vaccinations up-to-date as these feral dogs are not vaccinated and often carry diseases. No matter how friendly the other dog seems, we would not advise allowing your dog to have any contact as feral dogs often have mange and other diseases.

Chapter Fourteen
Getting Sick

As I mentioned in the chapter dealing with crime in Mexico, there are three topics which scare the average American when it comes to Mexico. The crime rate, the water, and medical care, especially for serious illnesses frighten many Americans. Everyone has an opinion about these topics, whether they have ever set foot across the border between the U.S. and Mexico or not. Usually, these opinions are steeped in rumor and innuendo. Many people say, "Someone told me that...," or "My brother knew someone whose sister heard from a third cousin that..." followed by a story supporting their opinion.

Becoming ill and having to seek medical care in Mexico is not difficult, scary, or guaranteed to result in horrific pain or torture. The only frightening issue I can think of is the language barrier — something that can be overcome. No one should avoid visiting or living in Mexico because of unfounded fears about the Mexican medical community.

If you expatriate to Mexico, eventually the need for medical care will rear its head. But, have no fear. Medical care in all but the most rural parts of Mexico is just as good, or better, than medical care in the United States.

If you live in No Place, Nevada where the only doctor is 900 years old and has never even seen a medical journal, you may not receive quality medical care. If the hospital (if there is one) looks like something out of a horror movie, you may not receive first-class care. The same goes for most of the rural areas of Mexico.

However, if you live in Los Angeles, Boston, or Chicago, you can expect top-rate doctors. You can also expect modern, well-equipped hospitals. The same goes for most large Mexican cities.

We think the key to healthy living in Mexico is adopting major preventive lifestyle choices. Eat right, exercise, and most importantly, reduce stress! Stress increases the likelihood that you will develop a major health problem like cancer, heart attacks, and strokes. Americans are dropping like flies because of obesity; sedentary lifestyles; fatty, high-calorie foods; and stress.

The climate in most of Mexico is conducive to healthy living. The weather is warm, but not too hot (except in the desert and in the tropics) which makes you want to be outside much of the time. When it is sunny, as it is much of the time in Guanajuato, we get out and walk. We feel great!

Another way to live a healthier life in Mexico is to adopt Mexico's worldview. Mexico still embraces the Judeo-Christian ethic, which America rejects. This is the belief that an infinite, universal, norm-giving God gives mankind normative ethics by which to rule his behavior. This belief says God is not only interested in the affairs of mankind, but also directs them.

Whether this offends you or not is not the issue. This is Mexico's worldview and is buried deep within its cultural consciousness. I, for one, hope the secularization which has routed God out of the American culture never touches Mexico.

This cultural worldview produces a wonderful saying which sums up its practical effect: "Ni modo. Esta en las manos de dios." (Never mind. It is in God's hands.) This is a most de-stressing, health-enhancing idea. You say it whenever you are tempted to get all bent out of shape over some stressor.

Here is another way to sum it up.

"During my Spanish lesson, I asked our instructor if Mexicans were afraid to fly commercial airlines. He looked surprised and said, "No. Always, as we board a flight, we cross ourselves, and put ourselves into God's hands. He alone determines when we die and we do not fear death."" (mexico-insights.com).

That, my friend, sums up the Mexican worldview. I think that is why we don't see the same cultural chaos in Mexico that prevails in the United States. Just think of the de-stressing effect of being in a culture like Mexico's culture. Stress kills!

People do become ill, despite their best efforts and intentions.

One lovely September afternoon after our Spanish classes ended, we decided to grab a bite of lunch with one of our classmates. Still new to Mexico, we were not too savvy about places to eat and places to avoid. We settled on a pizza place that sold pizza by-the-slice. The three of us were veteran pizza-by-the-slice eaters in the United States. We did not give our choice a second thought.

Chatting, we did not notice the pizza slices were in a

glass case, in the sun, being warmed by a 25-watt bulb. We assumed the pizza was fresh. That was our experience in America. Bad assumption

Our classmate and I chose hot dog pizza and my wife chose ham and pineapple. Hot dogs, for whatever reason, are a very popular pizza topping in Mexico.

Anyway, for about 87 cents each, we got a huge slice of pizza and a soft drink. It was an inexpensive lunch. We slurped and munched delightedly. Finally, we went to our respective homes to work on our Spanish homework for the next day.

About 2:30 a.m., the torture began. I spent the next six hours on the toilet with bucket in hand. You guessed it! The dreaded turista had paid me a visit. I was sicker than I had been in years. The last time I was that ill was when my roommate cooked us up a meal of 40-year-old Army rations...but that is another story. Finally, I was so dehydrated that my wife insisted I see the doctor.

Thus began my first adventure with the Mexican health care system. Boy, was I in for a surprise!

The doctor took one look at me, asked me what was wrong, and told me I would have to go to the hospital. Fortunately, the hospital is in the same building as the clinic, so I didn't have far to go. The doctor even helped me get from his office to my room.

I was in a private room complete with television, telephone, huge bathroom, a couch and chairs, and a cot so a family member could stay overnight. Everything smelled and looked clean. I later found out this was because someone came in twice a day to clean the room thoroughly, including the bathroom. I mean, she dusted, moved all the furniture to sweep and mop under it, and cleaned the bathroom from top to bottom. Incredible!

I was given a hospital gown and bundled into bed with

my wife's help. By then, I was as weak as a baby. Almost immediately, two nurses came in to take my vital signs and to get an IV started.

The nursing care was nothing short of astounding. There were always two nurses, and sometimes three, whenever they needed to do something. They were friendly, efficient, and tried to anticipate my every need. Unfortunately, they did not speak English and my Spanish, not good at that point, deserted my fever-weakened brain. However, we were able to communicate fairly well with many hand gestures.

The only major bump in the road between my nurses and I was when they repeatedly asked me how many times a day I was doing something. I understood the part about how many times a day I did something, but I could not begin to guess what that something was. I saw that these lovely women were becoming frustrated, but did not know how to get over this hurdle. Finally, they politely excused themselves (they actually asked permission to leave the room—isn't that great!) and had a whispered conference in the hall.

On their return, the head nurse marched up to my bed and asked, "¿Cuantas veces pee-pee, poo-poo cada dia?" I about blew my IV! The poor dear just wanted to know if I had had more diarrhea and if I had been urinating normally since I was dehydrated. After I left the hospital, I made sure that I learned the proper words for future reference!

My hospital stay was pleasant and restful. What impressed me most was that my doctor came three times a day to check on me! It wasn't just a 15-second visit either. He spent a long time with me each time, not just asking me how I was feeling, but how I felt about the care, the nurses, the hospital. When was the last time that happened to you in the United States?

They ran tests, dispensed medications, and gave me fluids by IV. By that evening, I was feeling much better. The doctor wanted to keep me overnight just to be sure I had no more diarrhea or vomiting and that I was hydrated again. It was a restful night, unlike nights that I have spent in U.S. hospitals.

The next day, the doctor dismissed me and told me to avoid eating pizza by-the-slice! I stopped by the administration office on my way out to pay my bill. Cringing, I waited for the clerk to give me my total—sure that it was going to exhaust my savings account. I was pleasantly surprised to find that all the tests, medications, doctor visits, nursing care, and overnight stay in a private room only cost $600 USD! That was the total out-of-pocket expense. That was not my co-pay or my 20%; that was my total bill.

If you expatriate to one of the established "Gringo Land" communities, you will have the advantage of excellent bilingual medical personnel. We have seen ads as well as telephone yellow page listings for hospitals and clinics that say their staff speaks Spanish and English.

Health insurance is on every potential expatriate's mind. There are various choices available.

Several insurance policies for travelers are available. Use an Internet search engine to look for companies that provide travelers' insurance.

Some expatriates have insurance policies from American companies. Some cover expenses outside the United States and some do not. Check with your insurance agent to be sure. We have talked with several people who have had problems. Many Mexican clinics and hospitals will not accept foreign insurance so you have to pay out-of-pocket. Then, when these people tried to receive reimbursement from the insurance company, the company denied the charges. Again, tell your agent you will be in Mexico and be sure your policy will cover you.

Mexican national health insurance is available if you have legal resident status. There is a six-month waiting period after you apply before it covers you and it does not cover some pre-existing conditions. However, for about $250 USD a year for a family, you can get major medical, dental, vision, and prescription coverage. You have to go to the government clinics and hospitals and you may have to wait for routine treatment. Some people have the national health insurance, but go to a private doctor for treatments the insurance does not cover or if they just don't want to wait.

Medications, as I have previously alluded to, are reasonably priced. Controlled substances, such as narcotic pain relievers, require a doctor's prescription. Otherwise, no prescriptions are required. Instead of going to the doctor, people sometimes just tell the pharmacist their symptoms and the pharmacist will recommend medications.

The advantage is, if you know your body and know what your doctor has prescribed for you in the past, you can ask for the same medicine if you develop the same symptoms. The disadvantage is you might misdiagnose yourself or forget to tell the pharmacist you are taking other medications which might interfere with what he or she recommends. Also, if you are seriously ill, it might be tempting to play doctor and self-diagnose instead of spending the money to visit the doctor first. For anything more than a cough, a stuffy head or an upset stomach, we recommend you see the doctor and not try to self-diagnose.

Now, this leads me to my next point. Many potential expatriates have expressed terror about going to the doctor and not being able to communicate in Spanish. That is a good point, don't you think?

First, don't get worked up into a tizzy over this. If you are in a "Gringo Land" community, there are going to be bilingual doctors. If you are in some of the smaller colonial cities, like Guanajuato, there are fewer English-speaking doctors, but there is likely to be at least one. Our internist speaks English (he did his residency in San Antonio, Texas) and we know of at least 2 other doctors in town who also speak English.

In a pinch, go to the local tourist office and ask if there is an English-speaking doctor. If not, ask if you can hire the services of an interpreter. In Guanajuato, we know several expatriates who are fluent enough in Spanish to be able to translate for you.

I firmly believe if you try to make healthy choices in your diet and exercise and make an effort to de-stress, you will be healthier in Mexico than you were in the United States.

Our advice is to get rid of the car and walk as much as possible.

Chapter Fifteen
Traveling Around and About

As you have no doubt divined by now, I have not mentioned owning a car as a wonderfully valid means of conveyance for a Mexican expatriate. There are exactly two reasons for this oversight. One is that I do not in any way regard car ownership as a wonderfully valid means of conveyance *anywhere*, and two, I hate cars and driving.

I know that is a hard thing to take coming from an American male, especially the part about hating cars. I do hate cars rather passionately and don't know which it is I hate most, driving or the car itself. They are death traps!

In America, probably every young man who approached the legal age to drive all but frothed at the mouth waiting for his 16th birthday to roll around so he could get his license. This is a rite of passage in America. I dreaded the day!

I turned 16 years old in the 10th grade. My father expected me to enroll in my high school's driver education course (can you imagine spending taxpayer's public education dollars on Drivers Ed in high school?). I was supposed to do as my older brother did the year before me and take this course; one I thought was a total waste of time.

I so dreaded driving that I was able to postpone taking driver's education until my junior year. It was then my father forced me to take the course to get my license.

I've always hated driving because of the nerve-racking concentration needed to keep from getting killed in traffic. I have always regarded driving as a kill-or-get-killed activity. I mean, driving requires almost an extraordinary effort to keep from getting maimed or mutilating someone else. To tell you the truth, I wonder why more people are not killed every day on the streets of America! I find nothing enjoyable about it whatsoever.

From the number of people who *are* killed each year on the streets of America, far too many Americans relax and enjoy themselves a bit too much when driving their death trap machines. While in their cars, Americans will do everything other than apply the needed concentration to their driving.

You've seen it, I am sure! People will read, apply their makeup, shave, and do their hair while driving. They floss their teeth, kiss, spank the children *who are in the backseat*, use the cell phone, all while they are supposed to be driving the damn car! They will do this in all manner of weather and traffic conditions. Just what is going on in their heads--anything?

What gets me is the average American's attention span and ability to concentrate has decreased to almost nothing! If you doubt this little piece of subjectivity, try this.

The next time you are at a stoplight, watch the driver directly in front of you. Notice now quickly he stops watching the thirty-second traffic signal to change from red to green and start doing something else. It is as though Americans have become incapable of concentrating for the insignificant time it takes for a traffic light to change.

They will, within a nano-second, start digging through their purses, dialing the cell phone, or taking some notes on a pad of paper attached to the dashboard. Or, and this one gets me, they will lean over toward the passenger side of the front seat and disappear from view altogether! Sometimes they will even break open a sack lunch and start lunching right there.

They can't concentrate long enough for a little traffic light to change. Yet, they are steering their multi-ton bomb (cars have a habit of exploding when crashing) to the grocery store. Do you see now why I've always hated to drive?

Let me say this, I have always had to have a car and have always had to drive while living in the United States. I attribute this to the fact of America's twisted idea of progress. It is virtually impossible to live anywhere in the United States and *not* own a car. Thanks to urban sprawl, everything that you need to get to is miles away from your home. The store, your family and friends, church, whatever, is so far away that you need a car.

Cars make you fat. Americans are fat and I am convinced it is because they drive everywhere and walk nowhere. Isn't this the truth? Here in Guanajuato, where car ownership is not as widespread as in the United States or larger Mexican cities, you will see a larger group of fit people. Why is that? People here walk! In a larger city, like Leon, Guanajuato, where there is more urban sprawl, people drive more; consequently, they are fatter. This was obvious in a recent visit to their American-style shopping mall. There were cars everywhere, and people there were fat like in America! Is there any doubt that car ownership makes you fatter?

One of the attractions that drew us to Guanajuato was that we would never, ever have to own or drive a car again! I can't tell you how happy that makes me. One of the side effects of our lack of a car is that we both, without even trying, have lost 40 pounds each and have kept it off. We continue to lose just because we walk everywhere. Though car ownership is unnecessary here, people still own them. I don't get it.

The cab and bus system is so well organized and cheap that if ever the near perfect weather goes south (if it rains) then we use the public transportation. We will walk the three miles to the supermarket and then cab back. I love this!

Traveling to another city is also easy and inexpensive. Occasionally, we have to go to a larger city to buy items that we can't get here. For example, we can't find the filter replacements for our water filter here in Guanajuato. So, it's off to Leon. We take the local bus to the Central de Autobuses (the bus station), buy tickets for the both of us for less than $10.00, and off we go. When we arrive in Leon, we take a cab to Wal-Mart then walk across the street to the mall. We find a restaurant we don't have in Guanajuato and eat there. We make a day of it. It's fun and relaxing. At the end of the day, we cab back to the bus station and go home. You might note that Leon is so big-- urban sprawl--that we are forced to use cabs (Leon does have city buses—we just have not figured out the routes yet). Walking would be impossible--progress?

We've also used buses to travel all over the country.

We've traveled two or three times from Mexico to the United States using Mexico's bus lines. The costs and conditions are cheaper and nicer than anything America has to offer. Bus travel in Mexico is a treat.

When I was a college student (too many years ago), I was forced to travel by bus. I can still recall the filthy bus stations and food guaranteed to cause a violent illness. I remember the curious mixture of smells (like an ashtray) and passengers who made me want to stay awake all night, or at least sleep with one eye open. Mexican bus travel is nothing like that at all!

The chief means of travel in Mexico is its elaborate bus system. There is not just one monopolizing bus company running the whole system. There are many bus lines doing what it takes to get your business. Wherever you want to go in Mexico, any one of its multiple bus lines can get you there cheaply. Bus travel in Mexico is affordable and it allows you to see the country.

In the Mexican bus system, there are different classes or levels of service, much like coach and first class in the American airlines. The buses have deluxe, first, and second-class service choices. These will, of course, have different prices. For example, my wife and I traveled to Puerto Vallarta for Christmas on the *ETN* bus line. This is the luxury class. It cost us 200.00 pesos, more than if we had taken the first-class *Primera Plus*. The luxury class has wider seats, climate control, and headphones for the movies they play (and one or two radio stations). It has a bathroom (one bus had two bathrooms), drinks and treats served by a steward as we boarded the bus, and was smoke-free. There was even a galley where you could make all the instant coffee and hot tea you wanted.

First-class buses have smaller seats, no headphones (the movies are blasted into the interior whether you want to listen or not), and there are no drinks, treats or stewards serving anything. Second class is sometimes called the *chicken bus* since you may have to share your seat with a chicken or goat. This is basic transportation from here to there. Sometimes you may even have to stand (that's happened to me!).

The bus terminals here are delightful! They are clean with wonderful antiseptic-smelling bathrooms. The bathrooms have attendants who keep them clean and fresh. The little cafeterias aren't bad either. We've eaten in them a few times. The food is good, not great, but a bit expensive. Most importantly, we've never gotten sick from eating in any of them. The terminals are comfortable with adequate seating for long waits.

Best of all, they aren't located in filthy, seedy parts of towns as are most American bus stations. Have you ever wondered about that? The bus station that I remember in Kansas City was located in such a dangerous area of town that it was anyone's guess whether you could get from the car into the bus station alive to catch your bus. Why do they locate bus stations in such areas of town in America?

If you want to see rural Mexico, then the second-class buses are your best bet. These buses are old and are just basic transportation. Many rural people (campesinos) come to town to work, shop, or see the doctor in these buses and then return at the end of the day to the farms or rural villages. These buses offer a rough ride. And, as I said, if there is no seating left, you get to stand, holding onto the bar. Comfort is not a consideration. These buses will take you where no deluxe or first-class bus dares to go. You may just share a seat, if you can get one, with a pig or goat.

For journeys between major cities, buy tickets on the deluxe or first-class buses. You will have to pay with cash (pesos). Round-trip fares are usually *not* sold. Unlike the United States, where if you buy a round-trip ticket, you will get a discount, you won't in Mexico. I haven't a clue why this is so. You buy your ticket "there" and when you are ready to come home, you buy your ticket "back". Make sure of departure and arrival times. Buses usually leave on time, but they may leave early.

Some guidebooks will caution against overnight trips on these buses. They cite *highway robbery* as the reason. Though this can happen in Mexico, it has also happened in the United States.

Some years ago, a senior citizens group took an out-of-state gambling trip on a charter bus line. On the way back home, somewhere in Louisiana, they were held up by *highway robbers*. This happened in broad daylight on the interstate system with cars zooming past them. Fortunately, one of the passengers had a cell phone and called for help. I don't know if the thieves were ever caught.

The first and deluxe class buses travel all the major toll roads, making robbery more difficult. My wife and I have taken several overnight trips and have never had an inkling of trouble. We have seen a huge police presence on these toll roads.

An idea to avoid bus fatigue is to break your trip up into parts. We know an elderly expat here in Guanajuato who takes trips back to the States in segments. He carefully books hotels, either on the Internet or by making phone calls, between here and his destination. Then he takes small, 5-hour trips and will stay overnight, or for a couple of days to sightsee in the smaller towns which he finds along the way. I think this is a grand idea, one that we never thought of, and are going to do in our future travels. It will sure prevent the sore backs and knees from long and difficult trips. Let's face it; whether you are flying, busing, or driving, you are worn to a frazzle having to sit for hours on end.

Now, on to my favorite subject--driving a car. You can drive around Mexico to see the country. Would I advise it? No, of course not. I cannot possibly give any advice other than the advice my friends have given me. We know this older couple, quite fit and full of vigor, who will drive literally everywhere in Mexico. They stay in small, inexpensive hotels overnight, then get up and tool around the country. It isn't something I would do, but it can be done and, as far as I know, they've not had any horror stories (yet) to report.

What scares me to death is the thought of the car breaking down in such a remote area that you are pretty much sucking eggs to get it repaired or towed to a shop. But, people do it, they adapt, and they survive. You will have to use your judgment.

Chapter Sixteen
A Time for All Seasons

When I was a small boy, I had no idea there were official starting dates for the seasons. How could I have known? No one told me. For example, March 21st is the official starting date for spring. I still, after all these years, am trying to figure out just who decided the 21st of March is when spring starts. How was this decided-by popular vote?

I was under the childish impression the seasons went as follows: fall began on September 1st, winter fell on December 1st, spring was March 1st, and summer began, of course, on June 1st. Don't ask me how I came up with these dates because I am 50 years old now and these were the musings of a 5-year-old.

I labored under this childish notion until I was eleven years old. Then, my thirteen-year-old brother decided that

I was ready to have this horrible mistake corrected. I denied his claim that I was wrong. It ended in a fistfight. He won. My seasonal dating methods were forever shattered.

I still protest the official starting dates for the seasons seem silly to me. I mean, really, who on earth can tell you when the seasons change? The planet doesn't keep a calendar nor wait for the official starting dates to click off, does it? The greening of the grass and the buds on the trees popping out tell you spring is here. The sound of returning migratory birds and their babies crying to be fed, the spring rains, and the increasing temperatures all conspire to tell you the season is changing. The calendar cannot do it.

Moving from the heartland of America (Kansas) to the heartland of Mexico (Guanajuato) has brought some seasonal confusion to me. This is par for the course since a great deal in my life confuses me, but that is another book.

In Kansas, nature would always give the clues the seasons were about to change. One did not need a calendar. The planet did just fine on its own, thank you very much. The shortening of the days, the leaves changing to yellows, reds, and oranges then falling to the ground all crisp and crunchy, the disappearing of the migratory birds all signaled that fall was here. All the seasons would trumpet their impending arrival with their clues and cues. It was like magic. In the heartland of Mexico, it is different. This confuses me to no end.

In Guanajuato, I am not exactly sure we have real seasons. I just don't know. For the longest while, I have been trying to figure this out. I keep waiting for the old clues from nature I knew from my childhood, but they are not forthcoming. A dry, crunchy yellow leaf, a massive departure of migratory geese screeching from the twilight skies, a snowflake, a budding leaf, some frost, anything would do.

My wife keeps telling me it is because we are now living closer to the equator and at a higher elevation so the weather patterns and seasons are a little different. She is probably right since she is a lot smarter than I am. Therefore, for the sake of argument we shall assume that she is absolutely right and I shall attempt a confused explanation of how the seasons work (or don't work) here in the heartland of Mexico.

Winter, if you can call it winter, seems to be somewhere in January and then only for about two weeks. Some would call December winter, but I don't think so. During both months, the nighttime temperatures can be 40-45 degrees Fahrenheit. On the surface, this can seem very wintry, wouldn't you agree? The Guanajuatenses (those from Guanajuato) shiver and shake half to death in this kind of weather. When we lived in Kansas, we would barely wear a sweater in those temperatures.

The kicker is that by day, during both of these months, the average daytime temperatures are a blistering 75 degrees Fahrenheit! Can you explain just how that is *winter?* Can you see how confusing this can be? On our first Christmas Day here we were running around in shorts and polo shirts. Can you believe that?

What does all this possibly mean? The nighttime temperature of 45 degrees Fahrenheit can most certainly be called a winter temperature, but what about the 75 degree Fahrenheit daytime temperatures? What do you call that? No one could argue that 75 degrees Fahrenheit is a winter temperature. Is it winter by night and spring by day? Where does the winter go during the day and where does spring go when it's night? Should we be calling it Wintspring, or Springwint? This is too confusing and I cannot understand it. I need help!

Here is what adds to my confusion. Birds still breed and produce young and most of the trees are still green and lush even though it is winter. Dogs still want to make puppies right in front of you while you are trying to walk to church during what the locals call winter--this isn't natural!

In our first year here, we totally missed spring. We were never able to figure out how or when it arrived. Since the daytime temperatures for the traditional winter months were always spring-like, we totally missed the transition from winter to spring, if there even was one. What we think is that spring begins in February, but we aren't sure. The daytime temperatures increase from 75F to 79F and the nighttime from 45F to 48F. Is this a nature cue? We simply aren't sure. Can one call this increase in temperature a transition from winter to spring? We just don't know.

If you think this is a little rattled, listen to this. Spring, and its official starting date, set by God only knows who, is supposed to be March 21st, right? March, April, and May are the hottest months of the year with traditionally summer temperatures. March will have highs in the mid-eighties and lows in the mid-fifties. April's highs are in the upper eighties and so are May's highs. The average lows for March, April, and May will be in the mid- to upper-fifties. So, what do we have here, Summer by day and spring by night? I live in seasonal confusion. I really do!

When mid-May rolls around, the temperatures are supposed to stay in the eighties through August. However, the rainy season starts. This lowers the expected average temperatures into the 70s with the lows in the upper 50s to low 60s. The rainy season ends sometime toward the end of September when the temperatures ease down into the high 70s until November when the temperatures become a freezing 75 degrees.

Where are nature's cues to the changing seasons? I think we left them behind in the United States. About the only cue you'll get the seasons are about to change is the arrival of the rainy season. It is rain of such a magnitude, by the way, that you begin wondering where you left the ark parked. If you are depending on the changing temperatures to tell you a seasonal transition is imminent, you can forget it. Basically, it is springtime all year round in Mexico's heartland. Some have called it Eternal Springtime (and indeed it is).

There are just a few types of trees here that do lose their leaves in the so-called winter months. At one park, I've even seen a few crunchy yellow leaves. However, where we live in the city, near the river in an area known as Barrio Pastita, the trees are just as green as they have been all year round. The rainy season brings out the green from a dull green to a brighter one. Otherwise, you couldn't tell the difference. And, there are plenty of birds in the trees and sky. They don't seem to migrate because they aren't stupid. They know when they have a good thing.

My Mexican friends refer to *winter*, or say, "I will go to the beach this *summer*." I don't get it. The seasons in Mexico are exactly two--Dry Spring and Wet Spring. It is springtime but dry, mid-September to mid-May and springtime but wet, mid-May to mid-September.

Some have asked if we miss the traditional four seasons. The short answer is no and the long answer is it was fun when I was young and could endure it. The changing of the seasons signaled something new was about to begin. It was exciting when I was a child. Now that I am fifty years old, eternal springtime seems pretty nice!

Though there isn't the excitement of seasonal changes

marking the advent of something new, there are seasonal events that do the job rather nicely.

Winter brings the celebration of *The Feast of the Virgin of Guadalupe*. This is bigger and noisier than Christmas. This takes place on December 12th. In Oaxaca, there is *The Night of the Radishes*. Although this conjures all sorts of funny and hysterical images in my mind, it is a very serious festival. Radishes are carved into various elaborate shapes and there is a competition where judges choose the best one. Again, I could really have a hoot with this one, but I shall restrain myself. There is, of course, *New Year's Day, Feast of the Epiphany, Feast of San Antonio Abad* (honoring livestock and pets all over Mexico), *Feast of Santa Prisca, Feast of San Sebastian*, and then lastly, *Dia de la Candelaria*. Goodness! These Mexicans will have a festival for just about anything.

If you find yourself wondering when springtime arrives in Mexico's heartland, look for the National Holiday celebrating the birthday of Mexico's beloved 19th-century president, Benito Juarez. In addition, a good clue is the celebration called, *Fiesta de la Primavera*. This translates to, "The Spring Party"--get it?

The arrival of summer is easy. June is *Navy Day!* (Mexico has a navy? What for?) June 10th is the *Feast of Corpus Christi*. June 24th is *John the Baptist Day*, which is actually a national holiday. Can you imagine the ACLU allowing the celebration of a national holiday honoring a figure from the New Testament to go unchallenged? Don't even get me started on that subject! July heralds the *Feria Nacional, the Guelaguetza Dance Festival* and the *Feast of Santiago*. Oh, I almost forgot, *Our Lady of Mt. Carmel Day!* Goodness gracious!

August has the *Feast of Saint Augustine, Feast of the Assumption of the Blessed Virgin Mary* and the *San Luis Potosi*

Patron Saint Fiesta. Can you believe all of that? Summer has arrived!

If you have any doubt that fall has arrived, watch for Mexico's *Independence Day.* This is in September. Then look for the mother of all festivals, *Cervantino*--a three-week-long celebration of the arts hated by the local residents, but loved by the merchants and artists. The city's economy thrives during that festival. Other events marking fall are *San Miguel Day, Feast of St. Francis of Assisi, Dia de la Raza* (similar to Columbus Day), *All Soul's and All Saint's Day, Anniversary of the Mexican Revolution, and the National Silver Fair.*

Therefore, if there is ever any doubt about what season you are in, just check Mexico's festival events.

Chapter Seventeen
Technology

I can't begin to tell you how much I love technology. When I was in the 6th grade, I couldn't wait for Friday nights to roll around so I could watch the original *Star Trek* with Captain Kirk, Spock, and Dr. McCoy. At that age (12 years old), I watched it, not so much for the story (although I did manage to memorize the dialog for each episode), but for the really cool futuristic technology. Some of that technology is no longer futuristic, but present reality. Have you ever noticed how today's cell phones look and act much like Captain Kirk's handheld communicator that he would flip open and give the order, "Beam me up, Scotty".

When Star Trek Next Generation, Voyager, and Deep Space Nine came on the air, I finally got into the plot and acting. But I still have to admit, each time someone fired a phaser, activated a transporter, or touched a communicator pin, that old thrill from my childhood would flood my emotions.

Two inventions which have to be the most impressive of the twentieth-century have to be the Internet and cellular telephones. But, as with all technology, Sci-Fi or reality-based, there is always the good, the bad, and the ugly associated with it. I don't mean with the technology itself. How can a cell phone jump out of your pocket and do something bad? What I am speaking of is the bad ways in which the users use technology.

If you've been jacked into the Internet for some time, the good, the bad, or the ugly will probably be very old news. Which of us hasn't received unsolicited e-mails advertising the most vile and shameful products like penis enlargement kits, plans, creams, exercises, drawings, written and video instructions? I mean just how much more gross can they get? "Amaze and astound your woman with your new tree trunk." "Triple your size." "Pin her against the wall." Need I go on? But, here is the deal: they would not keep trying to sell this crap unless it brought in revenue. People are buying this stuff or they wouldn't keep advertising it. The deceptive subject lines like, "Your ISP is being cancelled" would make me open these e-mails and suddenly, boom! There I'd have all I would need to know about penis enlargement, complete with before and after animated pictures. Most of these, I want to tell you, are American-based companies. Thank you very much, America.

Then, as if the vile porno isn't enough with which to cope, there are the get-rich-quick schemes. "Make your first million in just 10 short weeks!" Does anyone actually fall for this snake oil pitch? Just think of what that implies.

You would have to make $100,000.00 each week to make that goal. But people do buy into these scams or else no one would keep advertising them. They could not afford the costs of pushing their stupid schemes.

All the good of the Internet is too vast to cover in any book. However, something I adore is the wealth of knowledge you can access online from the comfort of your own home. Think of the time a writer can save in doing research. In the old days, when I needed to do some research for a writing project, I'd have to travel to a library (and you know how I love driving). I would have to find a parking place, wrestle with the card catalog, and then find the book. I'd have to read almost the entire book looking for perhaps a paragraph's worth of information and write it out by hand. Then it would be off to the next book to repeat the activity. I am exhausted just recounting the experience; imagine doing it!

Today, from the comfort of my own home (and especially now that I am in Mexico where there are only a few English-language libraries), I can access information in seconds. I can find the desired paragraph, then copy and paste it into my document in no time at all! Isn't that fantastic? You wouldn't believe how much faster a writing project can be completed using the Internet.

I can just hear a best-selling author and columnist, who apparently loves walking to his small New Hampshire town's public library to do research, bemoaning what I just wrote. If you are reading this, Bill, sorry!

The Internet is alive and well in Mexico. When exactly Mexico was wired with the Internet, I am not sure. About the closest I've come to a definite date is, "a few years ago"--a typical Mexican reply. Regardless of when *exactly* Guanajuato got online, it is hugely popular here. There are scores of Internet Cafés here in this city. Our best effort in counting them has revealed there are at least thirty. I am sure there are more in the various nooks and crannies of this wonderful little town.

While living in the United States, we had private Internet service in our home. This is still a rarity in the homes of Mexico since the cost of a home computer is still very prohibitive. We have Mexican friends who do have PCs and Internet service, but they are among the very few. Still, most of the users are kids who want to play the games and high school and college students doing research and typing papers.

The games and kids: a subject that causes my blood to boil and makes me run to take an extra Prozac. I have seen Mexican children, almost exclusively male, playing these American-produced and American-made violent games on the computer. I see kids as young as eight years old learning how to target and kill other people in these reprehensible games.

I once sat next to a young male who was playing a particularly violent game that used so much foul language. These games, mind you, are all in English. This is how these kids are learning their English. It had "f-you" and "mother f" in about every other phrase of the contemptible dialog. The child, in his excited frenzy of killing the bad guy in the video, would repeat the words he heard from the game's cussing characters. I was horrified and dumbfounded. I finally asked the child, in Spanish, if he knew the meaning of those words, to which he replied that he did not. What do you want to bet that he will soon learn the definitions? This is the legacy America is giving Mexico and the world.

Cellular technology is also here and I think here to stay. You can't watch TV without having a cell phone commercial blasting you between the eyes. In

Guanajuato's Yellow Pages, there are five companies offering cell phones and service as opposed to just three Internet Service Providers.

Cell phones are wonderful. I love these little compact communicators and had them when we lived in the United States. But, my reasons for having them is that my chronic illness, Fibromyalgia Syndrome, had the habit of hitting me with mind-numbing fatigue out of the blue, sometimes while I was driving in familiar territory. When I say fatigue, I mean that I literally can't think straight and become confused and disoriented. I would be driving down the street, one that I had traveled thousands of times, and, wham! I wouldn't know where I was or how to get home. That's when I would call my dear wife, who would faithfully and calmly talk me through the streets to a safe harbor. Isn't that pathetic? But, that is the nature of my illness. Therefore, I had a good reason for engaging my technology lust.

I think they are powerful tools for doctors, lawyers, judges, police officers, O.R. nurses, women, and teenagers who have to travel alone, the elderly, and more. But, what I don't get and cannot possible wrap my brain around is what do fourteen-year-old children (usually girls) need with cell phones? What possible emergency is out there that demands that tens of thousands (if not more) pimply faced young women need to be connected to the cellular network? I really, truly don't understand this at all! You know exactly what I mean. You see this all over American streets, malls, and schools: teenagers talking to each other on the phone or sending instant messages. I wonder why they don't have the phones surgically attached to the sides of their heads.

I want to know *why* these parents think that their child needs a cell phone. What logical reasons do these kids use to convince the moneybag parents to fork over the dough for these devices? What in these fourteen year olds' lives is so earth-shatteringly important that they need to cart their phones around? Can someone tell me this? It is Mom and Dad who are paying the bills, right? Maybe a completely new subculture of high-powered executive pimply-faced adolescents has arisen that we don't know about and they need to stay in touch to coordinate their plans for world domination!

My poor dear wife taught English to two classes of fourteen-year-old Mexican girls. All of them had cell phones. It was hideous. They all acted as though they were on emergency call for some dire situation that only their input could solve. These things would go off, all at the same time, while my wife was trying to teach these little sweethearts some English. This sent the whole lot of them crashing and diving into their purses for the phones. It turned out that these were nothing more than instant text messages from their peer cell phone users discussing boyfriend defeats and victories.

This leads me to my next point. Just why do they need cell phones in their lives? What is going on? Why do they need to send secret messages to the person next door, in the next class, or to the person who is sitting right next to them? Why? Why don't they talk to them at some convenient time after classes, on the way to the store or school, or over dinner? I fear for Mexico. This is Americanization of Mexico at its best. This is *American-* imported technology don't you know?

Listen to this: Cell phones in Mexico cost about the same as they do in America. Some Mexican households, who have interior phones in their homes, also equip themselves and their kids with these cell phones. I want to know how anyone, living anywhere, can afford to equip a family of four or more with cell phones. Why would you want to? Is not this a colossal waste of resources?

As I have mentioned in another chapter, I am absolutely passionate about going to the movies. I have been going to the movies since I was a child. It was a Saturday ritual in which I still often engage. It is my escape time. I have this bizarre and weird understanding about going to watch a movie that perhaps you will find a little strange. A great number of Americans and Mexicans do not share this understanding. What I understand is when you bother to travel to the movie theater, buy the tickets, get your crap-food from the concession stand; you are there to *watch* a movie. You are not there to talk, whistle, hum, have foreplay, or anything other than watch the damn movie! Does not the simplest logic dictate that this is how the whole thing works? You pay your hard-earned money for a ticket, you walk into this big room, hopefully with stadium seating, sit down, and someone invisible turns off the lights and starts the projector and you get a movie to watch.

Let's carry this logic a bit further. If you talk during the movie, a few events will occur. First, if you talk to your seatmate during the film, won't you miss some of the dialog and action? Won't you be preventing the person whom you are trying to distract with meaningless conversation such as, "Where are we going to eat after the movie?", or "Did you see how that vixen was dressed and the shoes she was wearing?" from hearing the film too? Won't the result be that you are now lost in the flow of the movie and will be forced to repeat the same distracting cycle when you ask someone, "What just happened?" It all ends up as a huge mess and a waste of your money and time. It is also the height of rudeness. So what does this have to do with Mexico and technology? Plenty!

At our very first movie at our favorite movie theater in Guanajuato, we were enjoying the action and dialog of the film. Suddenly, in the middle of the movie, I saw this strange and eerie blue, phantasm-like glow coming from two aisles over. It looked like a smoky, foggy, blue mist. I was thinking at this point, "Is this some special effect of the movie or what?" Distracted, I looked over to see what horror was about to devour us. Lo and behold, it was an entire row of kids (junior high to high school ages) with their blue, glowing cell phone screens sending text messages out into the world.

I do not mean to sound like a broken record, but I really, truly, swear to God don't get that! This happens in every single movie I've been to since then! Dear God, help me to understand this! Why pay money to enter a movie when you are not going to watch it? Besides, why distract other people, like me!

At first, I thought that it was because the movie was in English with Spanish subtitles. I thought that perhaps they were bored, didn't understand the movie, the subtitles went by too fast. Nope! That wasn't it at all. They do they same thing when the movie is in Spanish with English subtitles. What they do, apparently, is set their phones to *vibrate* when they get a call, but don't realize or care that the ghostly blue glowing screen bothers other people.

I love cellular technology dearly, but my heavens, give it a break when you go to the movies or when you are sitting in a classroom! I can't help wondering and I ask you, the reader, what importance have these people given themselves? Am I missing something?

Chapter Eighteen
How Long Will I Last?

Many gringos with whom we've shared our story of expatriating to Mexico have ended the encounter with something like, "Oh, we wish we could do something like what you did, but how long would we last?" I think that is an important and legitimate question. Could I last here for the long haul? How do I know if I have what it takes before moving to another country? Can I make it in Mexico?

The answer to that question is, of course, dependent entirely on you as an individual. The whole point of this book has been to get the potential expatriate to Mexico to *count the cost* and *be willing to pay the price* for expatriating to Mexico. As in any culture, I've tried pointing out there is the good, the bad, and the ugly. Can you cope with the not-so-good parts of Mexico? I don't know. Only you can answer that. The good news is that *you* get to decide. No one else can decide for you. There are several approaches that I might suggest that could help you figure this out.

One way is to come to the city in which you are interested and simply try it out. I've alluded to this elsewhere in the book. Don't make some huge commitment. Just come for a yearlong vacation. Come to test the waters. Arrange for someone to house-sit back home and try Mexico out for size. Take in all the good, examine the bad, and take a hard look at the ugly in this culture before making a huge commitment. If you love it, go back to the States, wrap up the loose ends there, and return to your new home in Mexico. If you hate it, then go home having had a wonderful yearlong vacation--nothing ventured, nothing gained.

Alternatively, you could make many short trips over a period of time. This is like trying it out for size a little bit at a time. This could be a slow and gradual absorption of the language and culture where you ease into it in your own time and way. You could try many different cities and locations before deciding for sure what you want.

On the other hand, you could do the shotgun approach. This is what we did. We sold everything we owned and moved. This isn't something we would recommend for everyone, but it worked for us. I think this would work more for those who have a less materialistic bent and who see their lives as more, much more, than accumulating the material crap they've been collecting all their lives.

This is, in fact, the first of the primary traits of a successful expatriate: The person who has little to no interest in acquiring vast amounts of material things--things that define the so-called American dream.

The second trait of the successful expatriate is to realize that just because Mexico is close to America, it does not imply there are similarities at all. This is the theme of this book: *Mexico is not America*! I am convinced, from our observations of American tourists and some of the expats who live in various locations, the majority expect more similarities than differences. If there are none, if they can't find the similarities they so crave, they go about turning the place they've chosen to settle in Mexico into a Little America--The Americanization of Mexico! Despite the *Gringo Landia* you see in various locations around Mexico, make no mistake: Mexico is a foreign country. Don't think otherwise.

I think, too, that most American tourists that visit the gringo tourist-trap cities believe that all of Mexico is one big English-speaking resort. Nothing could be further from the truth. If you want to be a successful expatriate here, you have to get it into your head that you are going to have to learn Spanish. All of Mexico is *not* like Puerto Vallarta, Cancun or other resort areas! My wife was once stopped on the street here in Guanajuato by an American couple all twisted into a knot and bent out shape. They asked frantically if she spoke some English. They were sincerely in shock that no one spoke English here. See what I mean? This couple expected all of Mexico to be like the resort areas where English is more widely spoken.

The third trait of a successful expatriate is being a flexible, roll-with-the-punches person. If that describes you, then you will be well on your way to becoming a successful expatriate. There are many punches with which the expat must roll in Mexico. We were in another city taking care of visa issues when I saw a typical and common scene. Some well-to-do-looking older woman, dressed in her carefully coordinated designer tennis outfit and dyed blonde hair, was buying a newspaper when one of the local beggars came up asking for a handout. This woman, in all her self-inflated importance, swatted at the beggar with her newly-purchased newspaper as if he was a mangy dog and said, "Vete" which means, "Get away"! Do you see why we don't live in that city?

If your blood pressure is sky-high when people don't show up on time for appointments or when you receive slow service, maybe you should not expatriate to Mexico. If you blow your top at the bad mail service, frequent power outages, or when you find dog poop on the sidewalks, Mexico might not be for you. If you cannot tolerate unbelievably loud festivals, waiting in lines that seem endless, or crowded buses, then think twice about expatriating here.

If not, and you can flexibly cope with these conditions, then this place could be for you! If you realize it isn't your place to criticize someone else's government or a mother's choice of food for her children, you are on your way to expatriating successfully. If you realize it isn't your place to criticize beggars who ask for hand-outs, or to judge the entire character of a nation based on the actions of a few, then you are one step closer to having the traits of a successful expatriate.

The fourth and last trait of a successful expatriate I want to talk about is one that is all-encompassing and is one that, if it is true in your life, absolutely assures you of being a successful expatriate. It is a trait that is sadly lacking in epidemic proportions in American society.

At the center of American cultural behavior is the notion that we are victims of our environment. That, if we turned out a bit, shall we say, emotionally challenged, that surely someone or something in our past or present environment is to blame. It is much simpler to hold someone else responsible for our woes.

The books lining bookstore shelves in the self-help

sections are full of these "you are a victim" books. People with more degrees after their names than the weather are telling us that our ruined lives are the result of the poor excuses for the human beings who dominated our past or are dominating our present lives. We are told if we are alcoholics, drug addicts, co-dependents, have anger control problems, have had five abortions or have been married six times, it certainly isn't our fault. There is someone else to blame.

This is America, folks! We are a nation of self-perceived victims who are constantly looking for someone or something else to make us happy. We are looking for someone else to rescue us from our misery and despair. We are an irresponsible and unaccountable lot, a nation of sheep, who are following the "You-are-a-victim" shepherd of popular psychoanalytic theory. Furthermore, we are following this claptrap so devotedly that we can't extricate ourselves from our collective depression. Let me say this: Mexicans, and I suspect the rest of the world, notice how miserable Americans are as a people.

Let me tell you what I am *not* saying. I am not saying that you are to blame for the abuse you may have suffered as a child, no matter the form it took. You, as a child, were not to blame for that which happened to you in the past. You are not to blame if some caregiver in your life sexually abused you, beat you, psychologically browbeat you, or whatever. You, as a powerless child, were not responsible in anyway for the circumstances visited on you. You had no power or control over your life as a child. You couldn't pick your parents.

Now, let me tell you what I *am* saying. I am saying that as a functional adult, you are responsible *now*, present tense, for how you react, feel, or think about those bad things which may have happened to you in the past or are happening to you right now in the present. Let's be honest. In this hideously imperfect world, bad things happen in the form of people and events, but as an adult, you are accountable for how you act *right now* to these events in your life.

Growing up, my siblings and I had to endure parents that no one in their right minds would have chosen. The atrocities these two people visited on us in their alcoholic and drug-dominated lives was a horror and, frankly, it is too embarrassing to recount the details. Suffice it to say there was every kind of abuse imaginable and then some. None of us escaped undamaged. Do you recall the movie *Sybil*, starring Sally Fields and Joanne Woodward? It was about a multiple-personality girl who had grown up with an abusive mother and passive father. Well, this story is mild and tame compared with what we endured at the hands of our parents.

The horror of my childhood was that it occurred when I was absolutely powerless and had no control over my life. I could not stop the abuse, the pain, the damage. I simply had to survive. I was *not* to blame for my parents' sin.

However, today I am responsible for how I choose to allow the past, all the memories, and all the pain, to affect me. As a thinking and choosing adult who is responsible for my own life, I don't have to allow anything or anyone from my past or present to control my emotions. As an adult, I refuse to give my power away to anyone or anything. Do you get this? Do you understand the point here?

No matter what may have happened to you, horrible as it was, today, right now, you and you alone get to choose how you are going to react to it. You get to choose the degree to which you allow *anything* to affect you! This is an empowering concept.

In life, from the time we get up in the morning until we go to bed at night, in our conscious moments, all we ever receive is information or stimulation. We receive a constant stream of stimulation or information all day long pouring into our lives. How we choose to react to that information is our choice. The information or stimulation is not an entity capable of making you do or feel anything. It is just there. It just comes. It just happens. You hear it and choose what to think about it. What this means is that no one can make you feel or do anything in response to the information you receive. It is always your choice! You and you alone are responsible for how you react to it. Always! So, what I am saying is that no one or thing in the universe can make you happy or sad. You alone choose happiness or sadness. All the things in the known universe ever supply you with is stimulation or information and you get to choose how you will react to it.

In the beginning stages of writing this book, I was asked by most of the gringos with whom I shared this book idea to be sure to include something about American politics. Ok, here goes.

The inevitable and highly predictable rhetoric at the end of the 2004 Presidential campaign went something like this: "This campaign has caused the country to become sharply divided." Oh, really?

All anyone ever received during the campaign was information. That's it, that's all. Whether it was Bush or Kerry in a political TV commercial, all you ever heard was information. It was neither good nor bad, it was just information. Neither Bush nor Kerry was able to make you feel or do anything. They just dispensed information. The information was not capable of making you feel anything either. It was just there. If you felt division with your family or neighbors over the information that was dispensed during the campaign, then it was how you chose to feel. If you felt divided against someone in the other political camp, then that was always your decision to feel that way. No one made you feel that way. All the 2004 presidential campaign provided Americans with was information and Americans need to take responsibility for how they chose to react to it and blame no one else. Take accountability, America!

Whether it is the past or present, if you are the typical American who *does not* get this important principle of personal behavior and accountability that no one or thing can make you happy or sad, then you are *not* expatriation material. You will not last in this Mexican world. If you think that people or circumstances have the power to make you happy or sad then forgot about moving to Mexico.

Mexico is a wonderful country that we love with all our hearts. We will stay here until we die or when Mexico decides she is sick of us and kicks us out. However, Mexico is not perfect. Like the rest of the universe, there is no perfect place in Mexico. It has good aspects, very good ones in fact, that Americans would benefit adopting into their culture. But it also has very bad aspects that it could stand to do without. But it is what it is. Neither you nor I can change it and I for one don't want to even try.

What I have been trying to tell you in this final chapter is that you get to decide about how you want to deal with all the stimulation and information Mexico has to throw at you. If you can choose happiness despite some of the quirks Mexico has to offer, then you will succeed rather nicely living here as an expat. If you do not accept responsibility for your own happiness, then Mexico is not for you. Mexico is what it is, nothing more and nothing less. It cannot make you happy or sad. The choice is yours about how you want to react to what Mexico is.

Mexicans revere that worth revering from yesterday, live entirely for today, and refuse to worry about what they can't alter or control--the future. This is the philosophy that will mark the successful expatriate.

ESSAYS

All of these contributing essays were re-printed with the kind permission of their authors.

The Older Language Learner
by
Mary Schleppegrell, Ph.D

Can older adults successfully learn foreign languages? Recent research is providing increasingly positive answers to this question. The research shows that: there is no decline in the ability to learn as people get older; except for minor considerations such as hearing and vision loss, the age of the adult learner is not a major factor in language acquisition; the context in which adults learn is the major influence on their ability to acquire the new language.

Contrary to popular stereotypes, older adults can be good foreign language learners. The difficulties older adults often experience in the language classroom can be overcome through adjustments in the learning environment, attention to affective factors, and use of effective teaching methods.

AGING AND LEARNING ABILITY

The greatest obstacle to older adult language learning is the doubt--in the minds of both learner and teacher--that older adults can learn a new language. Most people assume that "the younger the better" applies in language learning. However, many studies have shown that this is not true. Studies comparing the rate of second language acquisition in children and adults have shown that although children may have an advantage in achieving native-like fluency in the long run, adults actually learn languages more quickly than children in the early stages (Krashen, Long, and Scarcella, 1979). These studies indicate that attaining a working ability to communicate in a new language may actually be easier and more rapid for the adult than for the child.

Studies on aging have demonstrated that learning ability does not decline with age. If older people remain healthy, their intellectual abilities and skills do not decline (Ostwald and Williams, 1981). Adults learn differently from children, but no age-related differences in learning ability have been demonstrated for adults of different ages.

OLDER LEARNER STEREOTYPES

The stereotype of the older adult as a poor language learner can be traced to two roots: a theory of the brain and how it matures, and classroom practices that discriminate against the older learner.

The "critical period" hypothesis that was put forth in the

1960s was based on then-current theories of brain development, and argued that the brain lost "cerebral plasticity" after puberty, making second language acquisition more difficult as an adult than as a child (Lenneberg, 1967).

More recent research in neurology has demonstrated that, while language learning is different in childhood and adulthood because of developmental differences in the brain, "in important respects, adults have superior language learning capabilities" (Walsh and Diller, 1978). The advantage for adults is that the neural cells responsible for higher-order linguistic processes such as understanding semantic relations and grammatical sensitivity develop with age. Especially in the areas of vocabulary and language structure, adults are actually better language learners than children. Older learners have more highly developed cognitive systems, are able to make higher order associations and generalizations, and can integrate new language input with their already substantial learning experience. They also rely on long-term memory rather than the short-term memory function used by children and younger learners for rote learning.

AGE RELATED FACTORS IN LANGUAGE LEARNING

Health is an important factor in all learning, and many chronic diseases can affect the ability of the elderly to learn. Hearing loss affects many people as they age and can affect a person's ability to understand speech, especially in the presence of background noise. Visual acuity also decreases with age. (Hearing and vision problems are not restricted exclusively to the older learner, however.) It is important that the classroom environment compensates for visual or auditory impairments by combining audio input with visual presentation of new material, good lighting, and elimination of outside noise (Joiner, 1981).

CLASSROOM PRACTICES

Certain language teaching methods may be inappropriate for older adults. For example, some methods rely primarily on good auditory discrimination for learning. Since hearing often declines with age, this type of technique puts the older learner at a disadvantage.

Exercises such as oral drills and memorization, which rely on short-term memory, also discriminate against the adult learner. The adult learns best not by rote, but by integrating new concepts and material into already existing cognitive structures.

Speed is also a factor that works against the older student, so fast-paced drills and competitive exercises and activities may not be successful with the older learner.

HELPING OLDER ADULTS SUCCEED

Three ways in which teachers can make modifications in their programs to encourage the older adult language learner include eliminating affective barriers, making the material relevant and motivating, and encouraging the use of adult learning strategies.

Affective factors such as motivation and self-confidence are very important in language learning. Many older learners fear failure more than their younger counterparts, maybe because they accept the stereotype of the older person as a poor language learner or because of previous unsuccessful attempts to learn a foreign language. When such learners are faced with a stressful, fast-paced learning situation, fear of failure only increases. The older person may also exhibit greater hesitancy in learning. Thus, teachers must be able to reduce anxiety and build self-confidence in the learner.

Class activities which include large amounts of oral repetition, extensive pronunciation correction, or an expectation of error-free speech will also inhibit the older learner's active participation. On the other hand, providing opportunities for learners to work together, focusing on understanding rather than producing language, and reducing the focus on error correction can build learners' self-confidence and promote language learning. Teachers should emphasize the positive--focus on the good progress learners are making and provide opportunities for them to be successful. This success can then be reinforced with more of the same.

Older adults studying a foreign language are usually learning it for a specific purpose: to be more effective professionally, to be able to survive in an anticipated foreign situation, or for other instrumental reasons. They are not willing to tolerate boring or irrelevant content, or lessons that stress the learning of grammar rules out of context. Adult learners need materials designed to present structures and vocabulary that will be of immediate use to them, in a context which reflects the situations and functions they will encounter when using the new language. Materials and activities that do not incorporate real life experiences will succeed with few older learners.

Older adults have already developed learning strategies that have served them well in other contexts. They can use these strategies to their advantage in language learning, too. Teachers should be flexible enough to allow different approaches to the learning task inside the classroom. For example, some teachers ask students not to write during the first language lessons. This can be very frustrating to those who know that they learn best through a visual channel.

Older adults with little formal education may also need to be introduced to strategies for organizing information. Many strategies used by learners have been identified; these can be incorporated into language training programs to provide a full range of possibilities for the adult learner (Oxford-Carpenter, 1985).

CONCLUSION

An approach which stresses the development of the receptive skills (particularly listening) before the productive skills may have much to offer the older learner (Postovsky, 1974; Winitz, 1981; J. Gary and N. Gary, 1981). According to this research, effective adult language training programs are those that use materials that provide an interesting and comprehensible message, delay speaking practice and emphasize the development of listening comprehension, tolerate speech errors in the classroom, and include aspects of culture and non-verbal language use in the instructional program. This creates a classroom atmosphere which supports the learner and builds confidence.

Teaching older adults should be a pleasurable experience. Their self-directedness, life experiences, independence as learners, and motivation to learn provide them with advantages in language learning. A program that meets the needs of the adult learner will lead to rapid language acquisition by this group.

FOR MORE INFORMATION

Gary, J. O., and N. Gary. "Comprehension-based Language Instruction: From Theory to Practice." Annals New York Academy Of Sciences (1981): 332-352.

Joiner, E. G. The Older Foreign Language Learner: A Challenge For Colleges And Universities. (Language in Education Series No. 34). Washington, DC: ERIC Clearinghouse on Languages and Linguistics; available from Englewood Cliffs, NJ: Prentice-Hall, 1981. ED 208 672.

Krashen, S. D., M. A. Long, and R. C. Scarcella. "Age, Rate and Eventual Attainment in Second Language Acquisition." Tesol Quarterly 13 (1979): 573-582.

Lenneberg, E. H. Biological Foundations Of Language. New York: John Wiley and Sons, 1967.

Ostwald, S. K., and H. Y. Williams. "Optimizing Learning in the Elderly: A Model." Lifelong Learning 9 (1985): 10-13, 27.

Oxford-Carpenter, R. "A New Taxonomy of Second Language Learning Strategies." Washington, DC: ERIC Clearinghouse on Languages and Linguistics, 1985 (FL No. 015 798).

Postovsky, V. "The Effects of Delay in Oral Practice at the Beginning of Second Language Learning." Modern Language Journal 58 (1974): 229-239.

Walsh, T. M., and K. C. Diller. "Neurolinguistic Foundations to Methods of Teaching a Second Language." International Review Of Applied Linguistics 16 (1978): 1-14.

Weisel, L. P. Adult Learning Problems: Insights, Instruction, And Implications. (Information Series No. 214.) Columbus, OH: ERIC Clearinghouse on Adult, Career, and Vocational Education, 1980. ED 193 534.

Winitz, H. The Comprehension Approach To Foreign Language Instruction. Rowley, MA: Newbury House, 1981.

The Downside of Paradise

By

Bruce McCann

I've been living in Guanajuato City for over 3 years now. I'm quite happy here and the positive definitely outweighs the negative. One big thing that led me to Guanajuato was the fact that most of the streets in the center are pedestrian callejones and are too narrow for anything but foot traffic. Much of the motorized traffic runs through underground tunnels, leaving a large part of the center to pedestrians.

I remember my first impression around 5 years ago on my first visit when I got off the bus in a tunnel under the city center. It was the end of the afternoon in the month of January. After climbing the stairs to the street level, I walked around the center. The sun was blazing and the sky was a gorgeous blue. I quickly realized that if this wasn't paradise, it was probably as close as I'd get, at least weather-wise. I had been living in Brussels, Belgium since 1987 and feeling the warm, even hot, January sun in Guanajuato just did it for me.

I remember when I was researching places to live, no one ever talked about the downside of living in Mexico. And that's why I've decided to let you prospective Guanajatenses in on the few things I find bothersome about living here. They probably won't change your mind, but they might prepare you for what's around the corner.

Over three years ago, my wife and I bought a house around 10 minutes by foot from the center, up the hill from the University. Our house is located on a cul-de-sac and is comfortable, and the neighborhood is relatively quiet.

That said, one of the first irksome things I discovered is that the concept of "disturbing the peace" does not exist anywhere in Mexican law. And that Mexicans, unlike many Americans, never complain if the neighbor is making a ruckus at 2 am.

My neighbors across the callejon are decent, generally quiet people, but they have two little insufferable white poodles that bark very sharply at anything that walks by. Even their names are obnoxious: Poopie and Pongo. The neighbors let them out at around midnight to piddle before putting them to bed and they inevitably rush out of the front door barking like there's no tomorrow.

I have called the neighbors on the phone many times when this happens, asking them to please let the dogs out earlier, like at around 10 or before, so that they don't wake me up. I am always courteous on the phone. They usually say something like, "What can I do? They are dogs. Dogs bark. Why don't you try being more tolerant? In Mexico we are tolerant about such things." Like it's my fault I let myself be bothered by the noise! I've heard more than one story of noisy dogs simply being poisoned by the neighbors. As they say in Spanish, "Muerto el perro, se acabó la rabia"; a literal translation would be, "When the dog dies, he is cured of his rabies." I haven't yet gone that far because as a matter of principle, I don't believe murder is a decent way to solve problems.

Then, very recently, I discovered that there is a new state-run arbitration service called Justicia Alernativa in Guanajuato. I went to see them and they explained that their service is voluntary. In other words, they said, I can set up a meeting with the neighbor and a mediator, but if the neighbor is not interested and doesn't show up or refuses to come to an agreement, there is nothing they can do. So I decided to give it a try. Nothing to lose.

A few days later, I saw the man from Justicia Alternativa, Juan Carlos, slip the notification under the neighbors' door. A few days later, I got a call from Justicia Alternativa telling me I had an appointment the next morning at 10 with my neighbor and the mediator, the same Juan Carlos. The person I cited, Manuel, was not the one who showed up, but his brother who lives in the same house and who is (I'm not making this up) a midget surrealist painter, or maybe a surrealistic midget would be more like it. It turns out that Jorge, the midget artist, is the owner of Poopie and Pongo.

So Jorge, Juan Carlos and I talked for over an hour; the upshot was that Jorge refused to budge on anything and said his dogs' rights must be respected. I offered to give ground, saying I would go to bed later to allow him to let his dogs out later, but Jorge would have none of it. Jorge is half deaf and just doesn't understand how anyone could possibly be bothered by a barking dog. So I left feeling disappointed in humanity. Since then, I've been placing my faith in nobody and keeping my slingshot at the ready. When Poopie or Pongo gets noisy, I lean over my patio wall and shoot a pebble in their direction. They usually run to the back of the house and keep quiet. I think in time they will learn to associate their barking with my slingshot and get the message. In Mexico, you have to improvise your own justice because you can't count on the authorities.

A second thing I find a little less irritating and even sometimes amusing is the Mexican habit of telling lies or simply making things up. At times, Mexicans seem to want to tell you what they think you want to hear. But what they think you want to hear may, in fact, be very far from what you really want to hear, and even further from the truth.

Octavio Paz once said that Mexicans lie for three reasons: out of desperation, out of fantasy or out of necessity. If you ask your house painter why he showed up for work on Thursday afternoon instead of Monday morning as he promised, you should brace yourself to hear a tall tale, told with a straight face. You will probably ask yourself, "Can he really expect me to believe this cock-and-bull story?" After you hear 5 or 6 such stories, you begin to realize that it's of little use trying to expose him or call him a liar. Instead of getting all bent out of shape, I eventually learned to go with the flow. The same thing happens with plumbers, electricians, blacksmiths, etc.

If you move to Mexico, you will inevitably hire tradesmen, such as albañiles (masons), to work on your house. If you are lucky, like I was, you will find one who is reliable, punctual, honest and not too expensive.

My albañil does not work very fast, but he does good work and I figure anyone else would not be so reliable and honest, so I have stuck with him. He has done masonry at my house off and on practically since we moved here. When you work steadily with one in particular, he may very well turn to you when he is in a jam and needs a loan. That has happened several times already and my albañil has been very careful to keep to the repayment agreement. He recently asked me to lend him 5,000 pesos because his daughter was about to celebrate her 15th birthday, a major event in Mexico, and he had to buy all the food, drink and other stuff. I lent him the money, I was invited to the celebration and had a great time. He has since been paying me back faithfully.

The third thing I would mention is the practice in stores here of always serving the last customer to arrive. For example, I walk into a stationery store and I ask the girl for a ream of paper. As she turns to go get it, someone else walks in the door. "What do you need?" she asks, and goes to find what he has asked for. Then a third person walks in, ignoring all the other customers, and asks for a box of pencils, which she produces immediately and collects the money.

I guess the idea is to get all the people who walk in the door involved in a transaction so that they can't leave until it's finished, and in that way, not lose any business. But it's the opposite of how it works in all the countries I have ever lived in. Out of irritation, sometimes I call out, "Excuse me, I was here first!" and the shop attendant usually takes care of me immediately, especially if I am a regular customer.

Something else I learned early on is when you walk into, say, a hardware store, before you tell the shopkeeper, "I'll take that hammer", be sure to ask the price. Otherwise, the guy in the store may think "Here's another rich gringo; I can double the price and pocket the difference." I don't think that happens too often and it doesn't only happen to foreigners. The moral of the story is caveat emptor.

A fourth thing I genuinely find irritating is the bad habit of throwing garbage on the street. At various times, I have seen people, kids and adults, walking along the street and eating, say, a bag of chicharrones with chili sauce, or drinking a bottle of coke. Once they're finished, they simply put the empty bag or bottle down on the street or sidewalk and walk away. Once or twice I have told the person, "Hey, why don't you throw that in a garbage can?" On those few occasions, the person reacted sheepishly, picked up the garbage and took it away. But maybe he just threw it on the ground again when I was out of sight.

In general, I feel a lot freer here than I did when I lived in the States and especially in Europe, where the authorities are always on your back about something. In Mexico, people by and large leave you alone, but the other side of the coin is that the authorities do little to protect and help you. That would include the police if you call them to say your house has been burgled. Chances are they simply won't show up, or if they do show up and enter your home to have a look, they may well steal any valuables lying about when your head is turned. That is why everybody has to improvise their own protection by putting bars on their windows to prevent burglaries in the first place.

But Guanajuato is very quiet and mostly crime-free. Even so, there is some opportunistic theft. If you leave something lying around, it may disappear. A few years ago I hired a neighbor, a young philosophy student from Chiapas, to do some painting. He was painting the wall that runs around my property and at one point he had to climb down off his ladder and go get a rag. He hung his roller, dripping with yellow paint, on a rung of the telephone pole that stands on the callejon just on the other side of my wall. When he got back, the roller had disappeared. Somebody had walked off with it!

There were traces of yellow paint, which he followed hoping to catch the thief, but the trail eventually vanished.

I have no particular advice to give you except perhaps to take your time and enjoy yourself, take things in your stride. Oh, yes, learning to speak Spanish would be useful and would help you a great deal socially.

Mexico Living -- A Woman's Perspective
June 1997 Column

By

Karen Blue

Author of "Midlife Mavericks: Women Reinventing Their Lives in Mexico" available through Amazon.com.

Let's start at the beginning. The five most commonly asked questions before I came to Mexico were:

1. *Why not stay in California and retire?*
2. *Won't you miss your friends and family?*
3. *Will you be safe? What if there's a medical emergency?*
4. *What are you going to do with all your things?*
5. *What will you do with all that time? Can you continue to work?*

Why not stay in California and retire?

This question was posed most frequently by those who really didn't want me to go. Here were my two answers.

The first was that I couldn't afford to retire in California in the life style to which I had become accustomed. Using spreadsheets, it became apparent that even by moving into a cheaper house, getting a less expensive car, and generally cutting down on expenses; I would still need at least $4,500 pre-tax dollars per month to live. Remember, this was in Santa Cruz County -- the most expensive county to live in based on average income vs. average cost of living. I was nearly eight years away from tapping into my IRA moneys, and it would be yet another three years until Social Security kicked in. My investment income wasn't nearly enough to support me at that level for that long.

I could, however, live nicely on $1200 per month in Mexico with a maid and gardener. That amount was within my budget. Most single people down here live on $350 to $1500 per month. The average falls within the $800-$1000 range. (I'll talk more about cost of living and developing a spreadsheet in a future column).

The second reason was less pragmatic and more intuitive. All my friends would still be working. As it was, they had little time or energy left over for socializing. My other option for a social life would be the retired folks, who were too old for me and too retired. Okay, I generalize; but I wasn't ready for the old folks home. I knew that people who chose to live in another country would possess a certain amount of moxie. They would be risk takers and embrace change. They would welcome the differences and actively "live" their life. Don't ask me how I knew, but I did. And, I was right.

Folks down here have the time, the resources and the commitment to be active, involved and interesting people. There is a real sense of community and newcomers are welcomed with open arms. It's easy to find friends who share your interests and you have the time to invest in making those life-long friendships. In addition to diverse social activities, mother nature and the local culture provide many opportunities for artists, writers and those seeking spiritual growth.

Won't you miss your friends and family? Yes, of course. And I missed them when I moved to Washington, to Idaho and to Germany as part of my career. I made new friends, too. And now, with the Internet, it's possible to communicate daily with everyone I care about. And I have the time to keep in touch. In Ajijic, we still have to pay long distance rates to Guadalajara for the Internet, but that is expected to change this summer. Actually, we planned to have local access in April; but remember, we're on Mexican time down here. Manana, they say, doesn't really mean "tomorrow", it just means "not today!"

When you live in a beautiful country with one of the world's best climates (according to the National Geographic), your friends and family will visit you often. The International airport is just 30 minutes away. Most of my friends down here plan one or two trips back to the states (or Canada) annually, and welcome many visitors during the year. There's a great deal to do down here for your guests and it's much easier to have visitors when you have a maid!

Will you be safe? What if there's a medical emergency?

Safe? I can walk alone at night anywhere and feel safe. Yes, I lock my doors at night (unless I'm too tired to let the dogs out and then I leave one open for them!). Children play on the streets at night. They feel safe. I spoke to a beautiful young black woman who has seven children. She and her husband (an electrician) moved here after living in four different cities within the U.S. She says it's the first time she has been able to let her children out of her sight and not worry about their safety.

Mexico is a poor country and there are thefts. Leaving valuables displayed inside cars is not a good idea. Leaving keys in ignitions and leaving purses unguarded is not smart. Isn't this true just about everywhere? There are gated, guarded communities here. I don't live in one. I have neighbors who look after each other, and we pay for a neighborhood police patrol as part of our neighborhood fees.

In terms of medical emergencies; some of the best doctors, dentists and hospitals are in the greater Guadalajara area. Many "gringos" come down here because both drugs and operations are cheaper and medical care is excellent. Many kinds of insurance are available. I personally "flunked" the medical exam for the low-cost IMSS insurance because of high cholesterol. Shame on me. So, I continue to pay for private insurance which covers me in case of any major illness or injury. It also covers me for any emergency care required while I'm out of the country. Medi-Vac programs are available for those who want to be treated in their own country. Organizations such as the Lake Chapala Society provide help with everything from blood pressure checks to eye tests to arranging for the return of remains to the family

What are you going to do with all your things?

I'm one of those people who doesn't place a great deal of value on "things". I chose to sell or give away or donate most everything I owned. I brought with me about 1/3 of my clothes. There is no need for long johns and business suits down here! I also brought my grandfather clock (which came apart into three sections and could be packed in cartons), my photos, my computer and stereo equipment, personal items and my Christmas decorations -- five boxes of them. I had 30 boxes in all. After much research, I found that flying them down air cargo was the cheapest, safest way to get them here -- about $1500.

My friend Roseann shipped everything she had ever owned -- except for her 16-foot ladder and she regrets not bringing that! She's arranged her house exactly as it was in California. It cost her $7,000. I wanted new things and figured that I could totally furnish my house for less than it would cost to bring down the truck full of my belongings. I decorate with the local Mexican furnishings and artifacts; but if you prefer, we have beautiful shopping malls, Wal-mart, Price Club Sam's and Office Depot. There's really nothing you can't buy down here except licorice twists and

Mazda car parts! (More on bringing or buying cars in a future column).

What will you do with all that time? Can you continue to work?

My answer to this one was different before I came than it is today; and it will probably be different in the future. Since my job was one I could do from a "home office", it was both possible and desirable for me to continue to work part-time as a consultant. As long as I was paid in dollars and that money went into a U.S. bank account, I would pay federal tax; but no state tax since I reside in Mexico. No Mexico taxes would be applicable. If, however, I wanted to work for a Mexican company, I would need to get a work permit. Those dollars would be taxed by Mexico and not the U.S. (Disclaimer: I am not a CPA or tax consultant and this is grossly oversimplified, but it met my information needs at the time).

I needed to have that sense of continuity as I transitioned from a career to retirement. However, when I got here, there was so much to do and everything took so long. I realized there just wasn't enough time left in my life for work! I started volunteering at the local orphanage and put in a few hours a week of bookkeeping to help out a start-up company. I'm also writing this column and have published a few other articles. I guess that means I'm now a writer.

Several friends have taken jobs in the real estate business down here. Some have since quit and others have continued. Their decision seems to be based on financial need and/or values concerning time, contribution, recognition and identity.

America's National Culture on the Border
by
Jacob G. Hornberger, June 2000

People who rail that America's "national culture" is threatened by immigrants never explain which national culture they are referring to.

I recently visited my hometown of Laredo, Texas, which is located on our nation's Southern border. In grocery stores and department stores, half the signs are in Spanish and store employees greet people in Spanish. There are a few pizza parlors and even a Chinese restaurant, but they can't compare to the many restaurants selling enchiladas, menudo, chalupas, and tacos.

Laredo, which today has a population of 155,000, was founded in 1755 by a Spanish officer named Don Tomas Sanchez de Barrera y Gallardo, who named the town Villa de San Agustin de Laredo, after a town in Spain. Today, San Augustin Plaza is located a short distance from Laredo's two downtown international bridges, which connect the city to Nuevo Laredo, Mexico (population 300,000).

One of the major downtown streets in Laredo is named Hidalgo Street, after Miguel Hidalgo y Costilla, the father of Mexican independence. Another is Iturbide Street, named after Emperor Agustin Iturbide, the first ruler of independent Mexico. During my recent visit to Laredo, I noticed that the streets in a brand new residential subdivision had been named after coastal cities in Mexico, such as Puerto Vallarta.

After Texas won its independence from Mexico in 1836, Laredo refused to recognize Texas rule and for a time served as capital of the Republic of the Rio Grande, which consisted of a coalition of three northern Mexican states and southwest Texas, which were themselves revolting against Mexican rule, unsuccessfully. As part of the Treaty of Guadalupe Hidalgo at the end of the Mexican War in 1848, the war by which the United States acquired the northern half of Mexico, Laredo officially became part of the United States. (At the same time, Nuevo Laredo, on the other side of the Rio Grande, was founded by Mexican citizens who wanted to remain in Mexico rather than live in the United States.)

The long-established culture in Laredo has been one in which people informally converse with each other in either English or Spanish (or Tex-Mex, a peculiar blend of languages in which the conversants slip back and forth between English and Spanish, sometimes even within the same sentence). The local Spanish television channel and the Tejano (mixture of English and Spanish) radio stations seem to be at least as popular as the English-language ones. Generally, people are indifferent to the particular language being spoken, and everyone is accepting of those who speak only English, sometimes even marrying them (as my mother did).

But even the English-only crowd speaks a little Spanish when they visit what was once Mexico. After all, when was the last time you heard anyone say that he personally saw St. Anthony and, after traveling through the Pass, visited St. Francis, and ended up visiting the Angels (San Antonio, El Paso, San Francisco, and Los Angeles)?

Oh, did I mention that for more than 100 years, Laredo has had the largest bash in the country celebrating George Washington's birthday? Sixteen fun-filled days every February, including a grand parade with George and Martha Washington and their court in colonial garb on floats, the Society of Martha Washington Pageant and Ball, the Princess Pocahontas Pageant and Ball, Noche Mexicana,

Caballeros Cocktail Party, Streets of Laredo Jamboozee (including such musical groups as "Tommy and the Tomcats" and "Javier Molina & El Dorado,"), fireworks, street parties, and a fantastic Jalapeno Festival (including, of course, a jalapeno spitting contest).

If those who are dedicated to preserving America's "national culture" are referring to the culture in Laredo (which really is located inside the United States), they'll find plenty of support among the citizenry of this great American city located on the banks of the Rio Grande.

Mr. Hornberger is founder and president of The Future of Freedom Foundation (www.fff.org) in Fairfax, Va.

Printed in the United States
67409LVS00002B/98